NATIVE INSPIRING STORIES FOR KIDS:

A FASCINATING COLLECTION OF TRUE TALES ABOUT HEALTH, FAMILY, COURAGE, RESPONSIBILITY, AND RESPECT FOR NATURAL RESOURCES

A History Book to Inspire Young Readers About the Wisdom of Indigenous Tribes

ENNIS JEMMY

Table of Contents

INTRODUCTION

The Native Americans were brave hunters who followed animals like deer and buffalo to North America. They lived there for many centuries before Columbus came to the New World. There are many different tribes. Some tribes are the Apache, Cherokee, Chickasaw, Inuit, Iroquois, and Navajo. Each tribe has its own beliefs and ways of doing things. But even when they did things differently, all Native Americans believed in taking care of nature, being kind, and loving each other. Their beliefs and practices helped make America the country it is today.

A lot of the food we now enjoy was grown by the Native Americans. Things like corn, peanuts, potatoes, melons, and pumpkins were all grown by the tribes. Without the Native Americans, the Europeans would not have had anything to eat when they came to North America! Even the way the United States government works by dividing authority among different groups was inspired by the Iroquois tribe.

There are many fun ball games that we play today. Many people enjoy canoeing, tug-of-war, and relays. All these games came from Nativepeople. We are also taught in school about the importance of taking care of our environment. Even without the help of modern technology, Native Americans cared deeply for nature. They loved and respected all forms of life and only hunted for the things they needed. For them, caring for the environment was a way of life. A lot of Native American practices are still practiced by Girl Scouts, Boy Scouts, and during camping activities. The tribes were great at survival and very knowledgeable about the world around them.

The tribes were also great at communication. We use many of their words today. Some of these words include 'hammock,' 'barbeque,' 'skunk,' 'hurricane,' and many others. They even developed sign language!

Respect for elders was a very important part of Native American culture. Elders are the 'wisdom-keepers' of the tribes. They are served first when food is being shared, and it is considered rude to step in front of an elder in a line. Elders pass down the traditions and values of the tribe to the next generation. This is done through customs, social practices, ceremonies, music, story-telling, and art ("Native American Contributions," n.d.).

There are many famous Native Americans, with more appearing each day. Many of us know about Pocahontas, who even had a Disney movie made about her. We also have many brave chiefs, athletes, musicians, and even a vice president of the USA!

The story of the Native Americans is an amazing one that inspires many people. By following their example, we can learn to respect our environment, to be patient, to live healthy lives, and to accomplish our goals no matter what challenges we may face. This book has ten stories of wonderful Native Americans who helped others and had great adventures. Learning about them helped make me the person I am today, and I am sure it will help make you a great person too!

CHAPTER 1

How Susan Saved Her People

Friend, do it this way—that is, whatever you do in life, do the very best you can with both your heart and mind. And if you do it that way, the Power Of The Universe will come to your assistance, if your heart and mind are in Unity.—White Buffalo Calf Woman

Susan began to dream of becoming a doctor when she was just eight years old. Her father was a chief of the Omaha tribe. Susan's family and neighbors were not always able to get a doctor to see them when they were sick.

If I could become a doctor, Susan told herself, then I could help my people.

But this was many years ago, during the 1800s. There were a lot of female nurses, but not many female doctors in America. Most of the doctors were also white. Susan knew that she would face a lot of challenges if she was to pursue her dream. She would have to deal with people who did not believe in her. Some would even try to stop her. Becoming a doctor would mean that she would have to be very patient and study hard. Even knowing what she would face, Susan was determined.

Her father, Chief Joseph La Flesche—also known as Iron Eyes— was very proud of his daughter and her goals. He encouraged her to do her best.

"Do not let people put you down," he would say. "Go out there, attend school, and come out in the world as the best person you can be."

His words helped Susan to be brave. She knew no matter what, her father would always be there to protect her. His pride and support filled her with joy. Chief Iron Eyes believed that knowledge was very important. He knew that the world was changing and that his people would need to adapt to some of these changes. This meant following the path of peace. Chief Iron Eyes believed that Native Americans and whites should share with each other. That way, both groups would become stronger and smarter. He was a champion of change. His children learned and practiced Omaha beliefs, and also learned about the customs and culture of their white neighbors. They spoke Omaha, Otoe, English, and French.

The chief made sure that Susan had the best education possible. He had her tutored at home, and when she got older, he sent her to a school for young ladies. There, Susan learned how to walk, talk, and eat like a lady. The school taught her all about the Bible and Shakespeare. They showed her how to paint and play the piano.

When Susan returned home at age 17, everyone was very proud of her. She had become very knowledgeable. Susan became a teacher at the local school, but still, she did not give up on her dream.

"I still want to become a doctor," she said. She patiently taught at the school, all the while thinking about how to achieve her dream.

One day, Susan met an ethnologist named Alice Fletcher. Now, ethnologists were people who studied the way of life of different cultures. When Alice was sick, Susan helped nurse her back to health. Susan was so thoughtful and helpful that Alice was very impressed.

"You would make a wonderful doctor," Alice told her.

This made Susan smile. "I know, but medical school is so expensive. There is no way I would be able to go by myself."

"You should write to a group called the Connecticut Indian Association," Alice suggested. "They will help you."

"Even if I want to become a doctor, and not just a nurse?" Susan asked.

"Tell them how much you want to help people."

So Susan did. She wrote a long letter and sent it off. Day after day, she would wait, hoping they would help her. Finally, a response arrived. Susan was very nervous. Her fingers trembled as she opened the letter. After reading it, she cried out with joy. They were going to help! She was going to medical school to be a doctor!

Susan attended the Hampton Institute and then the Women's Medical College of Pennsylvania. School was hard, but it was exciting too. She learned all about science and the human body. While at school, Susan never forgot about her people. In her second year, she went back home to help everyone get better from measles. When someone wanted help, they would write to her asking for advice, and she would write back a response.

After three years, Susan graduated from medical school. She was at the top of her class, and gave the valedictorian speech!

Finally, it was time for Susan to return home to help her people. While at school, she met many people who were surprised at her dream. After all, women did not become doctors! Some said that she would fail. They thought that her tribe would not allow her to treat them at all.

"A woman cannot become a doctor," they would say. "Worse, a Native American woman!"

When people said that, Susan always had an answer for them. She even gave the answer in her graduation speech.

"I am proud that I am from the Omaha tribe," she would say. "The wisdom of my people will help make me an even better doctor."

Susan was right. Her heritage helped her to be kind, patient, and caring of those in need. It helped her achieve her dream and to work towards excellence no matter what. For Native Americans, the community is everything. Everyone worked together to help each other. They lived in harmony and provided support for anyone who needed it.

Native Americans also had no trouble accepting Susan as a female doctor. After all, many women in the tribes were healers. They believed that being physically healthy would also improve their spiritual well-being. True healing did not only help the body, but also the mind and spirit. It was a community effort, with families fully supporting those who were sick. Many ceremonial gatherings were held for the sick. Sometimes, these gatherings lasted days and weeks. The patients knew they were loved, that people cared and were willing to do what was needed to help them get better.

Elders in each tribe passed on their healing wisdom to the younger generations. This kept healing traditions and ceremonies alive for centuries. Their knowledge included how to use different herbs as medicines. They used these herbs to cure sicknesses of both the mind and body. The elders also shared many stories of healing. These stories helped give people a sense of purpose and belonging. It reminded people of the importance of their beliefs and practices. These stories also helped people to have hope and faith. By hearing about stories of healing, people were happy because they knew they could be healed too.

Native American healers were taught to be giving. They learned the importance of not being selfish. Native American healers were taught to look at things from other people's points of view so that they could better understand how their patients felt. They understood what it meant to struggle. This helped them show compassion and empathy to everyone. Healers learned to face suffering so that they would not turn away from others. While Susan learned about science at university, she learned the importance of living in harmony with yourself, your community, and nature from her tribe.

Balance was very important. In the tribes, healers chose daily to do good and worked hard to master the art of healing. During healing ceremonies, Native Americans would dance, play drums, and sing. This helped them to connect to nature and each other. It brought them a sense of peace and balance. People also gathered in groups to share and listen to each other. A spiritual leader would be in charge, and everyone would get a chance to speak. Native Americans practiced therapy long before science said it was helpful! (Rybaka & Decker-Fitts, 2009).

Susan used what she had learned in school and the wisdom of the tribes in helping others. She worked at a boarding school. Susan took care of the students and taught them about being healthy. She was so kind that soon people from the community came to see her too. Because she was employed by the school, Susan did not have to help them. Her job was only to take care of the students. But Susan never forgot her dream. She patiently treated everyone who needed her, no matter how tired she was. Sometimes, she worked for twenty hours a day! Everyone—both Native Americans and white people—wanted to be treated by Susan, and it was not long before she was the main doctor for over 1200 people!

Susan was more than a doctor to the community. She offered advice, taught people about their rights, and helped them write letters. She did not just stay in her office. Susan traveled all over the community to make sure everyone received medical care. It did not matter if it was raining or snowing. Susan would walk for miles, just to care for someone. When she had children of her own, she would sometimes bring them along with her, because she had no one to leave them with. Over time, she earned enough to get a horse and carriage to take her around the community. Sometimes, Susan would meet people who did not believe in her. They would refuse to take her treatment. But Susan did not give up. She continued to dedicate her life to help everyone.

Even though she worked hard as a doctor, writer, and lawyer for her people, Susan still wanted to do more. She pushed for healthy practices among her people and encouraged others to drink less alcohol. Like her father Chief Iron Eyes, Susan knew the importance of education. She made sure that children were taught all about health in schools.

Eventually, after writing many letters and collecting donations, Susan was able to achieve her greatest dream. She helped build the first hospital in the county! This hospital was opened in the reservation town of Walthill, Nebraska. Through hard work and patience, Susan reached her goals and helped many people.

Chapter Takeaway

- At just 8 years old, Susan saw what her people needed and decided how she was going to help. It does not matter how young you are. You can dream big and achieve your goals. Sometimes you may feel like you are too young to be of help. It is okay. You are the future. You can make little differences today and huge differences tomorrow.

- Susan faced many challenges. In those days, few people believed that a Native American woman could ever become a doctor. However, her father believed in her and never gave up on her. The world is big, and sometimes it feels very scary. Whenever you feel afraid or uncertain, just remember that your parents will always be there to protect you. They love you and will do everything to keep you safe. Your parents will support your dreams and help you become the best person you can be.

- The Native Americans believe that good health involves mind, body, and spirit. Our thoughts and feelings can affect our health. It is important to think positive thoughts. By keeping our minds on the good things in life, we are helping ourselves to grow and learn.

- When someone is sick, the entire tribe comes together to offer love and support. There is a famous saying that no man is an island. We need each other to survive. It is important to understand the value of family and community. A family and community that help each other will become stronger.

- Susan was very patient, even when people did not listen to her. We will meet a lot of struggles in life. We should remember our goals, and smile no matter what. In the end, we will achieve our dreams through hard work and patience.

- It does not matter who you are or where you come from. You can achieve greatness. You are smart, and you can become whatever you want to be.

- In the next chapter, we will talk about responsibility and water protection

CHAPTER 2

Chief Buffalo's Journey

Buffalo was born in 1759 as a member of the Ojibwe tribe. When he was a young man, everyone respected him. He was a great hunter and very athletic. Buffalo was able to feed many people in his tribe with his hunting abilities. He was very strong, and he could run and jump very fast. As he became older, his tribe realized he was also smart and good at speaking. Whenever Buffalo talked, everyone listened!

Eventually, Buffalo became the chief of his tribe. Even though he was from the Loon Clan, many Ojibwe people respected him and followed what he said. They called him Chief Great Buffalo and Great First One.

The Ojibwe and Dakota tribes lived close together. However, they did not always get along. Chief Buffalo believed that both tribes should be friends and gave a lot of speeches to the people. Soon, the tribes signed a peace treaty. This was very important, because a lot of Native Americans were losing their land. To save their history and their home, they needed to work together.

The Ojibwe had lived in the lands surrounding Lake Superior for many, many years. They called the lake *Gichigamiing*, meaning "great water." Several centuries ago, the Ojibwe had been living somewhere else. At that time, they had a lot more people and called themselves the Anishinaabe. There were so many people that no matter where you went or where you looked, the Anishinaabe would be all you could see.

Everyone divided themselves into groups, and each group had a job. Some fished, made canoes, picked berries, or carved wood and stone. Special people called the "planters of the Creator's garden" grew food. There was a lot of travel across the land,plenty of food, and everyone knew where they belonged.

One day, seven prophets visited the Anishinaabe people.

"You need to move to the west," the prophets told them. "Keep on going until you reach a place where food grows on water. If you do not do this, eventually all of you will disappear."

The Ojibwe talked among themselves and decided what to do. Not everyone wanted to leave, because they had a very good life where they were. Some believed the Creator had a special plan for them and that they should follow the wisdom of the prophets. After a lot of meetings, some stayed where they were while others moved.

They knew they had a long journey ahead of them.

"You will stop at seven different places," the prophets had said.

Each of the stops was at a place with a lot of water.

The journey took over five hundred years. Soon, the Anishinaabe came to a place they called Great Turtle Island because of its shape. The waters were clear, cold, and filled with a lot of fish. There was so much food that they stayed there for years. Some were happy, because they had stopped at a place with so many resources. However, others believed in the words of the prophets and wanted to continue. After a time, the Ojibwe broke away from the Odawa and Potawatomi people. They moved on to once again settle near water. The Ojibwe built large villages, organized huge war parties and held many ceremonies. Once again the group split, with some staying and others moving on. This happened several times until finally, the Ojibwe reached what they believed to be the prophesied place. They saw wild rice called *manoomin*, which grew on water.

"At last," they said, "we have found the place where food grows on water, just as the prophets told us."

This place was Lake Superior, and it was here that Chief Buffalo fought for the rights of his people. The Ojibwe had left their rich life and wonderful homes to journey for centuries to where they were now. Lake Superior's waters had nourished them for many years. They did not want to lose their prophesied home.

Chief Buffalo sent many letters to the government, but no one listened. One day, he decided enough was enough. He traveled all the way to the President to speak to him. By this time, Chief Buffalo was over ninety years old!

Chief Buffalo and several others were able to convince the President to give reservations to the Ojibwe.

"When you go somewhere new, you cut down the bad trees and leave the good ones," he said. "Please think of us as good trees, and let us live and grow on the land of our ancestors."

The Ojibwe not only got to stay on reservations, but they were also given money by the government for twenty years. However, many companies cut down the forests and dug up the ground. This made it hard for the Ojibwe to hunt for food. The waters of Lake Superior continued to provide for the tribe and helped them survive. The Ojibwe never lost their connection to the lake. The story of their migration was passed down through many generations. Each generation grew up with a deep love for water and worked hard to protect it.

Nibi (water) is the source of life and has a spirit of its own. Anishinaabe teachings call water the blood of Mother Earth that flows within and around all people, animals, and plants. The movement and power of water are significant to Native Americans. Water is patient, and can change mountains over time. It sustains life both in itself and on land. Water cleans not only the earth but all who live on it.

Throughout the centuries-long journey of the Anishinaabe, water was a constant part of their lives. They journeyed close to rivers and streams where they could fish, travel, and purify themselves. Water played an important role in many of their ceremonies. At the final destination, it provided the sacred wild rice that they had journeyed so long for. While on the shores of Lake Superior, the Ojibwe were able to trade with other nations.

Like Chief Buffalo and many others, Ojibwe today are engaged in activities intended to protect their land and its water sources. They are always fighting against pollution. In 2003, a group of Ojibwe women walked for 1300 miles around Lake Superior to raise awareness of the importance of protecting water. Just like the first journey centuries ago, this walk was inspired by a prophecy. An elder predicted that after 30 years had passed, the water would be too dirty for anyone to use it.

"One bottle of water will cost as much as a piece of gold," the elder said. (Thompson, 2003).

When the Ojibwe women heard this, they knew they had to do something. Women and children have a special connection with water. Children grow in their mothers' bellies which have water. Because of this special connection, women are called the Keepers of Water. It was their job to keep the water clean and to protect it. Women also sing songs during ceremonies about the importance of water. They use water to care for their home and remind everyone in their tribe of what to do to keep their water clean.

The walks have gone on for several years. Other women reached out to different tribes to come together and stop projects that are harmful to water. To this day, they keep companies from running oil pipes on their land. There are even workshops that teach children about the importance of keeping a balance with the environment and protecting the blood of Mother Earth. Both Native men and women are always doing whatever they can to keep their waters safe.

Chapter Takeaways

- Chief Buffalo believed in making peace with those who you are fighting with. People do not always get along. Sometimes they fight. When someone does or says something to upset us, we should choose to take the path of peace, and encourage those around us to do so. We are stronger when we work together

- Chief Buffalo was over ninety years old when he went all the way to talk to the President. Our age does not stop us from doing great things. We could be as young as Susan or as old as Chief Buffalo and still make a difference in this world. Even though traveling so far must have been difficult for Chief Buffalo, he still did what was needed to save his people. And he was successful! There is a lot that we can do when we are determined.

- Even though the Ojibwe were living a wonderful life, many of them traveled for years and years just because they were told to. Sometimes, we have to move even though we do not want to. It is never easy, and we leave many things we love behind. But everything has a purpose, and we should look forward to what we will meet when we reach where we are going. The Ojibwe started over and created another wonderful life in a new place. No matter where we are, we can be happy. All we have to do is have faith and put in the effort.

- Water is very important. We drink it, bathe in it, and use it to clean, and heal. The Native Americans have always treated water with the care and respect it deserved. Even without science, they knew just how important it was. We should also take care of water. Remember, do not throw garbage in it. Turn off pipes that are not being used.

- Many Native Americans are working hard to protect water and to get people to do what is right. Taking care of water is the responsibility of everyone. It is our duty, and we should do it to the best of our abilities. We could join in programs that educate people about water protection. We can talk to our friends and families and remind them to treat water right. Without water, there would be no one on earth.

- In the next chapter, we will look at family love and ceremonies.

CHAPTER 3

~⌇~

Buffalo Calf Road Woman and Dull Knife

The stories of the Native tribes include many brave men and women who fought for their families. One of these women was called Buffalo Calf Road Woman. She was a member of the Cheyenne tribe in the 1800s. She was a strong warrior who saved many people and helped make other warriors feel brave.

Once, there was a major battle where many men came to attack her village. They had strong weapons and were led by a man named General Crook. The Indian men from the village went to defend themselves from these attackers. However, when they saw how many people were coming, and how many weapons they had, they slowed down. They knew they had to protect their families, but they were not sure that they could win. Still, they fought, even though they were afraid.

While the other women stayed in the village or watched from afar, Buffalo Calf Road Woman went right into battle. In the middle of the fighting, she saw that her brother had fallen off his horse into a gully. Soldiers everywhere were coming after him. When she saw this, Buffalo Calf Road Woman knew she had to save her brother. She rode right up to him, pulled him onto her horse, and rode away!

All the Cheyenne warriors cheered when they saw what she had done. Her bravery made them feel braver too. They fought hard against the soldiers, and soon they won. All the soldiers who were left ran away. The warriors were so happy that they praised Buffalo Calf Road Woman. From then on, they called her Brave Woman. They even named the battle after her! To this day, whenever anyone speaks of the fight, they call it 'The Battle Where the Girl Saved Her Brother."

That was not the only time Buffalo Calf Road Woman saved someone in battle. She did it again the very next week in another fight. A young warrior fell from his horse and she rode in to rescue him. Once again, her actions inspired the tribes to fight harder, and they won that battle too.

Buffalo Calf Road Woman married another brave warrior named Black Coyote. After she had given birth, she would still go out to fight with the baby tied to her back!

One day, the soldiers came and attacked the village. The Native Americans had to run away to safety. Even though Buffalo Calf Road Woman was pregnant, she still fought hard and defended all the children. When the tribe tried to return home, Buffalo Calf Road Woman was there defending them all the way. She never gave up on helping her people, especially her family.

Even though she was a woman, Buffalo Calf Road still risked her life to protect those she cared about. For Native Americans, family was extremely important. Growing up as a Cheyenne woman, Buffalo Calf Road learned about the strength of family bonds. Each individual home was where a Cheyenne child first learned about the rules and traditions of the tribe. This knowledge helped them to grow and become a useful part of their society. Each household had parents, aunts, uncles, grandparents, and children. Everyone had their duties and they all worked together to take care of each other. The Cheyenne believed that a strong, loving family would lead to a strong, loving nation. Not only did family members have duties to one another, they also had responsibilities to the tribe as a whole. Everyone had to do their part for the tribe to prosper. Otherwise, problems would start to appear in the tribe. Buffalo Calf Road Woman was a dutiful Cheyenne girl. She wanted to contribute more to her people, to help them in any way she could.

Another strong Cheyenne warrior who did everything for his family was Dull Knife. He was a great friend of Buffalo Calf Road Woman and her husband. They defended their families together many times. Like Buffalo Calf Road Woman, Dull Knife also saved his sibling from harm. When he was just nine years old, his family got separated from the rest of the tribe during a buffalo hunt. His parents were busy, so Dull Knife and his sister played together by the stream.

Suddenly, there was a loud noise. All the buffalo that the tribe had been hunting came running toward the family! Dull Knife's mother was so frightened, she jumped up into a tree. She was too far away to get her children to safety. It was up to Dull Knife to save himself and his sister. He did this by grabbing her hand and running to a little cave that some beavers had built. The brother and sister hid there while all the buffalo ran past. When their parents found them, they were very happy. His father and mother told him he was very brave.

Dull Knife grew up to be very brave and resourceful. He helped feed his people when they were hungry and guided them when they were lost. Eventually, they made him the chief of the tribe!

Once, his brother got hurt in a fight and none of the warriors could get to him. Just like Buffalo Calf Road Woman, Dull Knife took a horse and rode to his brother's rescue. His act inspired the other warriors who followed him. Together, they saved Dull Knife's brother.

Buffalo Calf Road Woman and Dull Knife were just two examples of Native Americans who did everything for their family. The chief, elders, and warriors all thought of their families first when making decisions. To them, it was very important to keep the families of the tribe safe and healthy.

For many tribes, 'family' included more than just the people around them. It also included everything on earth. So plants, animals, and other humans were all seen as family. As such, they all had a responsibility to each other and were expected to care for and protect each other.

The idea of family among the tribes goes beyond blood relation. Often, friends and neighbors within a tribe come together to make extended families. Sometimes, a child can have a second set of parents. These parents are chosen at birth. This ensures that the child is well-taken care of. If a child gets sick, there is always someone ready and willing to step in and take care of the child.

Men, women, and children were all considered to be very important. The men were the main hunters and warriors. Some were responsible for clearing the fields for the women to plant. They used the trees they cut down to make houses, fences and canoes. Many men also fished. Some of the women of the tribe were also warriors. A majority were gatherers, who collected berries and nuts to eat. The women were also crafters, who made bone weapons and tools. They took care of the home and skinned and cleaned animals to cook.

In the Dakota tribe, the man would leave his family to live with his wife's family. The Dakota saw women as the source of life. These women were the caretakers of the home. They decided on each member's place. This included where each person slept, sat, and their roles in the family. While there were set roles for each gender in the tribe, sometimes both men and women would take on each other's duties. This was considered normal. Every contribution was welcome because it meant the tribe would become stronger. Every person was also seen as equal.

Children are very precious to Native Americans. They are the future and are cared for and educated by everyone in the family. Everyone in the tribe was excited when a woman got pregnant. The women would stop doing any activities they thought would be harmful to the baby. They also stopped eating some food. Both the mother and the father would visit the medicine man regularly. They would also wash their hands and feet every day. A pregnant woman did her best not to argue with anyone or think negative thoughts. Everyone around her treated her well and tried to make her happy.

The Navajo tribe would hold a ceremony called Blessing Way when a woman was pregnant. This ceremony lasts for two days. There was a special chant that the tribe would say. The Blessing Way helped make sure that only positive things would happen to the mother and child. The Navajo also used this ceremony when a girl entered puberty, to bless the home, and to heal sickness.

The tribes did whatever they could to make sure the baby was born quickly. They would say special words or give the pregnant women special things to drink. Some women had their babies alone, while some had other women around them. Many babies were born close to rivers and other places with water. The act of giving birth was considered to be a ceremony by the Native Americans. Once the child was born, the entire tribe celebrated for several days.

Giving a newborn baby a name was also very, very important to Native Americans. To them, all things in life had a name. A person's name told them who they were, and what their purpose in life was. For the Ojibwe people, the mother and father would bring tobacco to the elder when looking for a name for their child. The elder would smoke the tobacco, and then the child's name would come to them in a dream. Afterward, there would be a big celebration with plenty of food. The elder would talk to the child, telling them their name and what it meant. The tribe believed that the child heard and understood the elder. Afterward, the elder and the child had a special bond and called each other by a special name.

For the Sioux tribe, babies do not get their names when they are born. Instead, they get nicknames. As they grew up, their name was added to. If they did brave things or were good at a skill then they received good, strong names. If they did bad things then their names would be weak. Each nickname that they got described their personality and the things they have done. Some people receive names after they have become adults.

The elders and grandparents were especially important in raising children. They were the ones to pass on the traditions, stories, and wisdom of the tribe. Children were seen as mini-adults and were given roles in the family. The boys learned their responsibilities from their fathers, while the girls learned from their mothers. The children would follow their families around and watch what they do. Sometimes, they would ask questions and the adults would answer. Instead of giving them tests and quizzes, the adults would allow the child to do the tasks themselves. If the child did it well, then they knew that the child had learned. If not, then that meant the child needed to continue watching their parents and learning.

Native American children did not receive harsh punishments. When they did something bad, they got serious looks from the adults around them. If the bad behavior continued, they would be scolded in front of the entire tribe. However, they were not spanked. The tribes believed that, while it was important to discipline children, it should not be done in a way that would crush their spirit. The adults wanted their children to be proud and strong.

Family was important to the Native Americans. Each tribe had special ceremonies that showed how much they loved and celebrated each other. Everything they did, they did to protect the ones they loved.

Chapter Takeaway

- Your family is the first connection you have. They are the ones who care for you and teach you how to behave in society. Every family member has a duty to each other. You should all love, care for, and support each other. Having a happy family will help you to grow strong and kind.

- When you are making decisions, it is important to think about your family. What you do can affect them. When you do bad things it will hurt them, even if you think it will not. Similarly, when you do good things it makes them happy.

- Your parents love and care for you. People have been celebrating the births of children for thousands of years. Children are special. Without them, there is no future.

- You can be brave like Buffalo Calf Road Woman and Dull Knife. When you see your family members or friends in trouble, you can stand up for them. You are all stronger together.

- Everyone in the family has a part to play. You might be small, but there are lots of things you can do to help your family. Even things that you think do not matter will help make your family stronger and happier. You are valued and loved.

- In the next chapter, we will look at kindness and hospitality

CHAPTER 4

~⌒~⌒~

The Great Chief Tamanend and William Penn

C hief Tamanend belonged to the Lenni-Lenape Indians. The name Lenni-Lenape means "original people." The Lenape are often called the Delaware Indians today. Chief Tamanend was so wise, brave, and kind that both Native Americans and Europeans respected him. They called him "the Affable One," which meant that he was friendly and very easy to talk to. He was the speaker of his village and many people respected what he said.

Tamanend was born around 1628. His people were both hunters and farmers. They fished in the river and hunted deer and beavers. They also grew squash, beans, and corn. The Lenape tribe lived in smaller groups made up of family units. Each group would move around when they had used up all the resources of the place where they were staying. They also had their own way of making laws.

Family units normally had between 50 and 100 people. Each unit would form a village. The villages were temporary. They would only stay in an area until the firewood and other land resources were used up. After it was used up, they would move to another area. By doing this, they made sure that the land they lived on would have a chance to regrow its natural resources. Preserving the land was very important to the Lenni-Lenape.

The small size of the villages and the emphasis on preserving the land's resources meant that there weren't great numbers of the Lenni-Lenape. Their small population was easily maintained by hunting, fishing, and farming. The small population also meant that the government of the Lennape could be less formal than other tribes. Each village was run according to the wishes of all its members, and a sachem (speaker) was chosen to represent the collective wishes of the village. The sachem would interact with other villages, making sure they respected the wishes of their whole village.

At first, Tamanend didn't have much power over the government of all the Lenape villages. He was a sachem for his own village, and as such, he only represented their interests. But, he had a friendly personality, was gentle with others, and was honest in his dealings. As such, he built influence among other villages beyond his own.

The Lenape tribe had three clans. These were the Turkey, Turtle, and Wolf clans. Tamanend became the Chief of the Turtle Clan. The Turtle Clan represented the great turtle that emerged out of the ocean to provide the land that has become North America. He earned respect with his honorable behavior, resulting in him gaining more power. Through the reputation he built as an honorable individual and chief of the Turtle Clan, Tamanend was chosen as the representative of all three clans when dealing with Europeans.

The land on which the Lenape lived was granted to a white man named William Penn by the King of England. The king did not actually have a right to give the land to William, but he acted as if the land was his anyway. To prevent fighting, William Penn and Chief Tamanend had many discussions with the Lenape and their representatives. After a long period, the two formed a treaty.

William Penn was also known as a man of honor. He sought to build a common understanding with the Native Americans on the land the English King gave him. He tried to learn *Unami*, the language of Chief Tamanend. William did not intend to interfere with the way Native Americans governed our tribes. His intention was to create an honest agreement where he would gain permanent ownership of the land. This attitude helped when forming the peace treaty, because Tamanend could see he was a man to be trusted.

The treaty would guarantee that there would be peace between the people represented by William Penn and the people represented by Chief Tamanend. The treaty meant that William Penn had to give things like blankets and kettles to the Lenape so that he could take and sell their land. Chief Tamanend said that the Lenape would live in love with William and his descendants while the water runs, and the sun, moon, and stars shine.

This treaty was honored by both individuals and the people they represented. Peace reigned in the land for more than 75 years. This was thanks to the wisdom and hospitality of Chief Tamanend and his people. He did not desire to cause fighting, but rather to create peace. Because of his wisdom, many celebrated him as the patron saint of America.

Despite the success of the treaty, later things became problematic. The Lenape weren't materialistic, meaning they didn't attach a lot of importance to material wealth. Rather, they valued freedom and security. Their way of life was important to them. As such, the treaty to give away land in exchange for material objects was not in the best interests of the tribe. Despite this, they abided by the treaty as best they could, claiming other rights when they were needed.

Today, Tamanend is honored by the Tammany Hall building. It's a big building in New York City. The top of the building is made of glass and metal. The glass and metal is shaped to look like the back of a turtle. This is to represent the connection between Chief Tammanend and the Turtle Clan.

St. Tammany's Day is celebrated on May 1st of each year. It's a particularly important festival date in the state of Pennsylvania. Pennsylvania is the state that formed around the land that was part of the original peace treaty, particularly the land of the Lower Bucks and Central Bucks counties. The purpose of this day is to promote the values of harmony, honesty, and honor.

Chapter Takeaways:

- Chief Tamanend of the Lenni-Lenape people was a brave man who showed wisdom. He pursued peace rather than war and he always extended a friendly personality to those he didn't know.

- The Lenni-Lenape form of government is informal. A sachem (speaker) is chosen for each village. The sachem makes decisions based on the votes of all in the village. When dealing with other villages, the sachem shares the opinions of their village with the other sachems. The joint decisions of a group of sachems leads to an inter-village agreement. All the villages follow the joint agreement.

- William Penn was a British man who had been gifted the land that is now Pennsylvania and Delaware by the king of England. He was an honest man who wanted to make a safer place for people of his religion (the Quakers).

- Tamanend was the most influential, friendly, and peaceful of all the sachems. He was chosen to be the main negotiator with William to buy Lenni-Lenape land. They formed a peace treaty that sold the land to William in exchange for items such as blankets, kettles, and guns.

- The Lenni Lenape didn't have an idea such as personal property, so they didn't understand the long-term effects of the treaty properly. This caused problems after 75 years of peace. Despite these problems, the Lenape would remain as peaceful as they could when fighting for their rights later on. They were influenced by the peaceful legacy of Chief Tamanend.

CHAPTER 5

~~~

Growing Up and the Story of Herman Lehmann

Your birth is the starting point of life. It is a sacred point of your life and will define your identity. The government will ask you about your date of birth when you fill out legal documents. Your date of birth will be used by companies when you work with them. Your friends and family will keep a record of your birth date so they can celebrate your birthday every year.

Because it is so significant, many cultures have special practices related to birth. In Native American tribes, there are many rituals that are followed, depending on what tribe you're from. These practices have the purpose of making your birth as pain-free and calm as possible.

The Mohawks and Mahikans share similar rituals when it comes to birth. The Mohawk tribe is part of the Iroquois Confederacy. As a tribe, they respect bravery. They believe there is honor in putting yourself in harm's reach when doing so for the good of all. They have a history of being fierce and capable warriors.

The Mahikans are a tribe that originally come from the upper parts of the Hudson Valley in New York state and surrounding areas. The name of their tribe means "the people of the waters that are never still." They have a long history of moving from place to place after they left their original homeland. They crossed many bodies of water and large areas of land until they established their new homeland. Their new homeland was in a place where the waters were never still and were always moving. The Mahikans are a part of the Lenape Indians (now mainly known as the Delaware Indians).

Both the Mohawks and the Mahikans practice giving birth by themselves. In other words, a mom is normally by herself when she gives birth. She finds a place along a river or stream. The place is sheltered with mats to make sure the mom and her new baby are both safe. Once they've made a safe place, the mom waits until the baby is ready to come out. Mohawk and Mahikan moms are known to give birth easily.

This type of birth ritual is how the Great Peacemaker, Tekanawita was born. The Great Peacemaker provided the calm that was needed during the troubled times of the Five Nations of the Iroquois. During this time, people wanted revenge for the bad things that had been done to them. Rather than work through their differences and give forgiveness, people wanted to get back at those who had wronged them. As a result, the entire society has become difficult to live in.

Tekanawita lived during this time of great troubles. He saw that the only way to make the world a nice place for all to live in again was to create peace. He created an agreement for all the Five Nations in the region to live in harmony with one another. This agreement was called the Great Peace. The nations planted a white pine tree to represent the Great Peace, and they buried their weapons in the ground around the tree. The Great Peace was put together in such a wise way that when Canada and the United States were being formed, the Founding Fathers looked to the Great Peace as inspiration about how to put together the governments of both countries.

Before giving birth, it is expected that a new mom will be strong. If she is strong, then she will be able to struggle less when giving birth. Expecting mothers are supported by other women in their community while they're pregnant. If they have questions about what to do, they can ask an older and wise woman for guidance. If they need assistance with directions about the birth procedure and how to take care of their newborn, they can ask a woman that has taken on the functions of a midwife in the community. While new mothers need to be strong, they can rely on the other women in their community to help them gain the strength they need.

When a woman is giving birth, most tribes don't allow men to be present. Giving birth is seen as a job for the mother, and on some occasions, there would be a midwife of some female family members present. The birth is often done over a pile of leaves. The pile of leaves is a soft place for the baby to fall on when they come out of their mom's body. The leaves and earth upon which the baby falls can be seen as Mother Earth welcoming the child into the world. Mother Earth is seen as the life-giving being and force in many Native American cultures, so her presence at birth is important.

There are steps taken in many tribes to prepare the mom's body for the process of giving birth. Avoiding some types of foods and being on a special diet is one of these steps. Being less active while pregnant so that the baby isn't jostled around and injured during pregnancy is another step. There are also some teas that mothers drink to ensure the birthing process is fast and smooth. Tea used by the Cherokee for this purpose are Partridgeberry, Blue Cohosh, and black cherry tea. The Koasati make a tea of cotton plant root to ensure that giving birth is pain free.

Some things the pregnant mother is taught to avoid are neckerchiefs and standing too long in doorways. Neckerchiefs might lead to complications with the baby when they come out. It could lead to the baby having breathing difficulties from things being wrapped around their neck. Standing in doorways too long could make giving birth a slow process. It's as if the baby will be stuck in the doorway between the mom's womb and the outside world.

If the baby is having difficulty coming out, an older woman in the family could be asked to come help with the birth. She would try to frighten the baby out of their mother's womb. The older woman would tell the baby that she's coming to the baby and that they should come out before she catches them. In some tribes, the words used to help with this are very specific.

The Navajo make the process faster by giving the mom a sash belt. The sash belt is put over the branches of a tree for the mom to hold onto. This makes it easier for the mom because she has support from above. It also makes it easier for the child because pressure from above and gravity from below are used to help the child come out.

We hear stories of warriors and great chiefs every day. They are brave and they are wise. But what many of us don't realize is that our mothers are some of the bravest people in the world. Giving birth isn't easy and it takes a lot of preparation. Our mothers make sure they prepare well so that it's as easy and as healthy as it can be when we are born. There aren't many great legends told about giving birth, but it's a part of life that takes a lot more bravery and endurance than many others. Our mothers deserve our respect for going through this process of giving birth with so much strength and dignity.

There are many ceremonies followed after giving birth to make sure that both the mom and child recover quickly. One of these is putting the child in the cold water of a stream every day for the first two years of their life. This makes sure the child is clean. It also helps the baby build up strength against the elements. The baby's hands and feet are given special attention when washing because these are more likely to get dirty than other parts of the body.

The mom normally takes on her daily tribal duties soon after giving birth. This makes sure that she forces herself to become strong again. She doesn't lie down for weeks or months on end. By becoming active she contributes not only to her physical health, but also to her mental health. It's also important for the mom to see that she's not only a valuable person to her child, but a valuable person to her whole community.

An important tradition in many tribes is a welcoming ceremony for the newborn. These ceremonies help the child feel more at home in their new surroundings. They also bring the family and community together as a support structure for the child. The ceremonies make sure that the child is welcomed into the community in a way that's connected with their heritage and culture. The child is given the honor of being made part of the community in the same way their mom and dad were.

A practice that is followed in some tribes (such as the Navajo) is to use a cradleboard in the first few months. This is a type of carrier used to keep you safe while you sleep as a baby. In cases where your mom uses it, she will be able to work while you sleep if a cradleboard is used. Before putting you in it, she first wraps you in a blanket so that you're nice and snug. She then puts you in the cradleboard so that you're safe while you sleep. By using this, she makes sure that your back is protected and made strong and straight.

A Native American baby spends most of their time with their mother. Due to cradleboards, their mom can take them with them when she goes to work. When the baby gets hungry, she would feed it milk and then let it sleep again. When the baby gets a bit bigger, they spend time around their mom by playing or resting close to where she's working. When they get a bit older, a child will follow around their parents and imitate the work they do.

A boy will stay with his father during the day. He will watch him to learn how his dad hunts and how to do his other jobs. When he's a bit older, he will practice doing the things his dad does. A girl will follow around her mom and watch her to see how she does her work. She will try to copy her mom so that she learns how to do her work. If a boy or girl acts naughty, their parents don't spank them. Rather, their parents will describe the naughty actions in front of the entire village.

Herman Lehmann

Herman Lehman was a German boy who became a Native American warrior. He was born to a German family in Texas. His family decided to settle near Fredericksburg. There were many German families that moved to the area to set up a life in Texas. German settlers bought land from a German organization or from the government of the Republic of Texas.

One day, while he was working close to his parents' house, he was taken. He was taken by Apache warriors. They had seen him and his brother in a field and took both of them. His brother escaped, but he remained with the Apache. He thought he would never be able to see his parents again. He was taken to his new adoptive father.

The great Apache leader Carnoviste was to become his adoptive father. Carnoviste was strict with Herman. He expected Herman to learn the ways of the Apache. By learning the ways of the Apache, Herman would be able to become a valuable member of the community. At first Herman didn't want to learn the Apache's ways, but later he changed his mind.

He learned the language of the Apache. He learned how to hunt and how to fight for his new tribe. They taught him how to gather and capture food too. All the things he learned allowed him to become a strong and confident young man. Soon he was joining other warriors to protect the villages and people of his new community.

An Apache community that didn't get along with his own took his adoptive dad away from him. In return, he took away the medicine man of the opposing community. Times were difficult for Herman, but he used his training to remain tough. He found a Comanche community. They were impressed with the work he had done with the medicine man of the rival Apaches, so they took him in.

He became an active participant of his new Comanche groups. He helped their warriors. He also helped their hunters. The rules he learned while growing up as an Apache helped him in this new community. He lived and worked with them for a few years. The Comanche band he was a part of eventually broke up and Herman was moved away from his community to Fort Sill in the Indian Territory.

The head of the Comanche, the great Quanah Parker, helped Herman when his band broke up. He became almost like a new adoptive father to Herman. Quanah Parker was a leader of the Comanche that was first a warrior chief, and later became a peace chief. Chief Parker spread the importance of peace throughout the Comanche tribe. He became the first person to be a leader of all the Comanche.

Quanah Parker helped Herman get some land so that he could have his own home. Herman stayed on that land until it was found out who his birth parents were. Eventually, it was discovered that his birth parents weren't lost, so Herman was sent to live with them. He would miss the Apache and Comanche ways while learning the German ways of his birth family.

He became a productive member of the German community of Loyal Valley, Texas. He got married and had children of his own. However, he never stopped loving the ways of his adoptive families. He would continue practicing some of the ways of the Apache and some of the ways of the Comanche for the rest of his life. His niece tells how he used to love sharing stories of his adventures as a young boy in the Native American community.

The story of Herman shows that you have the ability to be successful in whatever group you're a part of. If you learn the ways of your group and you participate in its activities, you will have a positive impact in your group.

Chapter Takeaways

- Birth is one of the most important parts of your life. It's the moment when you come into the world. People from your community meet you and welcome you. There are different ways to welcome a baby into the world depending on your cultural traditions.

- Mothers need to be strong to give birth. They get training from other women in the tribe so that they know what to do. When the time is near, depending on what tribe they're from, they follow certain practices to make the birth easier.

- After birth, the baby is introduced to their village. The newborn stays with their mom during the first few months or years. When they are still too weak but their mom is ready to work, the baby is kept in a cradleboard. This way their mom can work while they rest.

- As they become bigger they play and sleep around the place where their mom works. Once they are a child, a girl stays with her mom to learn how she does her work. They watch her and try to copy her. When a boy becomes a child, he stays with his dad to look at what he does and to try and imitate his actions. As a result, Native American children quickly become capable individuals who know how to work around the village.

- Herman Lechman was a boy born to a German settler family. He was taken to live with the Apache tribe where he learned their ways and lived according to their customs. Later he lived with the Comanche tribe and learned their ways. He was a capable warrior and hunter in both tribes.

- He was moved to Fort Sill in the Indian Territory. There he was adopted by Quanah Parker, a chief that advocated peace.

He stayed there until his German family was found, at which point he was moved back to them.

- He struggled to learn the German ways, but understood them eventually. Despite living in a non-tribal community, he kept many of his Apache and Comanche customs throughout his life. The way he had been raised had left a permanent impact on him. He loved the Native American way of life. Even when he became an old man, he continued to tell stories about the years he spent among them.

CHAPTER 6

⌒‿⌒

Coming of Age–What It Is and the Tale of a German Boy Who Became a Native American Man

T he child is responsible for learning about their tribe. They need to listen to the stories of their elders. They need to hear about the history of their tribe and understand their tribe's beliefs. When present at ceremonies, they need to pay attention so that they can learn the rituals that are performed. They will need to perform the same rituals some day.

Some of the important rituals to learn are religious ceremonies, such as those that honor ancestors. These rituals bind the community together. By knowing them and participating, a child helps to strengthen the ties that bind the whole community. The lifestyle of a child is continued until they're ready to come of age.

Coming of age normally takes place between the ages of 14 and 17. Once you've come of age, you need to complete the ceremony that's specific to the customs of your tribe. After that ceremony, you're seen by the community as an adult. When you're considered to be an adult, you're expected to act like one. You're no longer allowed to act like a child.

Coming of age ceremonies depend on your tribe. The Apache perform the Sunrise Ceremony. Another name for the ceremony is *Na'ii'ees*. It normally takes four days to do. This is a ceremony for girls who have become women. The girls will be told when they are ready to do it.

The Sunrise Ceremony requires six months of teaching. After the teaching has been completed, the ceremony can be done. The teachings show what the Apache spiritual values are. It also shows what the Apache cultural values are. Learning about the history of the village, and the tribe as a whole, is an important part of the process. They are also taught about the Earth, how it is made up, and where they are on the Earth. As these girls become young women, they are expected to learn a lot of information that is needed for them to make decisions as a responsible member of the community. This includes information about the first woman, Ísánáklésh.

The ceremony itself includes a lot of dancing. There is also running and chanting. Praying is an important part of the ritual. The girl doing the ceremony is painted with a combination of clay and cornmeal. When the ceremony is completed, she blesses the whole tribe. She also goes to individual members of the tribe to help them heal.

The Yankton Sioux tribe have a similar ceremony (called *Isnati Awica Dowanpi*) for girls that are becoming women. It is also four days long. The girl doing the ceremony is taught many things such as how to relate with other people, how babies are made, and how to keep a healthy mind. They are also taught skills they will need as a woman. This includes how to use beads, how to make jerky, and where to gather herbs, fruit, and flowers.

When a girl is doing this ceremony, she may not feed herself. She may only be fed by other women in her camp. She must stay in the camp for the entire ceremony. She stays in a tepee that she raises herself on the first day. She gets bathed in sage water to absorb its healing powers and to wash away things that are not good for her. While she undergoes the *Isnati Awica Dowanpi,* many ceremonial songs are taught to her to sing.

One example of a coming-of-age ceremony for boys is that of the Inuit on Baffin Island. It is done when a boy is about 11 or 12 years old. They are taken for hunting with their dad. Their dad will teach them how to hunt. He will also help his boy get more comfortable with the cold weather of the Arctic. This ceremony is now also done with Inuit girls.

As part of this ceremony, the boys and girls are taught numerous things. They are taught about the community they live in. They are also taught traditional skills. This is best done in camps that are away from the settlement where the boy or girl lives. As part of the ceremony, a shaman is asked to improve the communication between the boy or girl and animals. This makes it easier for them to hunt.

The Vision Quest is one of the most common coming-of-age ceremonies. It's also done at other points of a person's life when you go through a big change. The purpose of the Vision Quest is for you to interact with your guardian spirit. Your guardian spirit is your supernatural teacher. They often show in the form of an animal or a human-like animal.

Your guardian spirit will give you advice. They will also show you answers to questions you have and questions you didn't know you have. Often the advice they give will be in the form of a song. Many people have said that their guardian spirit helped show them their life goal. The connection they made with their spirit guide helped them for the rest of their life. Many adults have said their spirit guides protected them through times of challenge, hardship, danger.

In many tribes only boys and men do the Vision Quest. In some, women and girls also do it. The reason women and girls don't always do it is because the changes girls go through as they become women are very clear. A girl goes through changes every month starting when she's around 11 years old. These monthly changes show that she is ready to go through her own type of ceremony.

In most tribes a person will need to do the Vision Quest before they advise others spiritually. The function of a shaman is to relay the messages of the spirit world to the humans, who live in the physical world. As such, shamans need to seek guidance from their own spirit guide first. Once they've been given their own path, and when they have found answers to the questions of their lives, shamans are better equipped to advise others. Your shaman will be able to provide you with better answers about nature, spirits, gods, and God. They can often also help you with healing and medicinal plants.

When you do a Vision Quest, there are many ways you can contact your spirit guide. The ways used vary from tribe to tribe. Often you will first get instructions from your shaman or a religious person before you do your quest. The methods used to contact your spirit guide include prayer and fasting. Fasting is when a person stops eating food or eats less food for a period of time. Fasting helps a person to focus on the spirit instead of the body.

While you're on your quest you will most likely go somewhere far from your home. This place will normally be in the wild. While you're there you will be expected to find your own food (mainly plants). You will be taught how to get your plants and how to find water before you start the quest. Sometimes you will be given special types of plants that give you stronger visions.

You won't always see your spirit guide. If you don't see it at the time you begin the process, it's best to end the quest. Your quest teacher will tell you more about this. You will know that your quest is successful if you have seen specific types of animal behavior, if you find an animal-shaped object, or if you have a dream in which your spirit guide appears. All of these could be signs from your spirit guide. When you've seen your sign, you go back to the camp or you go back home. When you're there, an elder will help you decide what the sign means.

Richard Wagamese

Richard Wagamese is a successful writer and storyteller. He is of Native American descent. He's an Ojibwe and grew up with the Ojibwe ways. The Ojibwe tribe is very large. There are many members living all around the Great Lakes. The tribe is known for its association to living by lakes and the importance it attaches to rice as a source of food. The prophecies of the ancient Ojibwe instructed them to move west to where they could find food growing in the water. This is the reason they attach so much importance to rice as a food source.

The connection with the water goes beyond growing rice. Canoes are also important in this tribe. They are used to get around and to fish. Fishing is also an important part of the diet of the tribe, alongside rice, other plants, and some hunted animals. Their connection with water is not the only thing that makes the Ojibwe unique. They are also known as generous and spiritual people.

Gift-giving is one of the major traditions of the Ojibwe. They like to empower other community members and also people outside their community. They do this by giving presents or being helpful.Generosity is so important to the Ojibwe, because they understand they can either use spiritual forces for good or for evil. By choosing to use spiritual forces to aid others, they can safeguard the health of everyone.

While many spiritual beliefs and traditions are widely shared among the Ojibwe, are privately held by individuals. This means that some beliefs are agreed upon by almost everyone in the tribe. It also means there are some beliefs that are held by a single person that they don't share with others. These personal beliefs are normally gained through their connection with their guardian spirit, a connection that is built during the Quest.

The Vision Quest has been used for many generations as a way for each person to determine their own journey in life. It also gives people the chance to build their personal values and see how important those values are to living a good life. Overall, the spiritual understanding, moral values and survival skills each person learns on the quest makes them more valuable members of society.

Richard Wagamese was raised by a foster family. For this reason, he did not learn the Ojibwe traditions as a child like other youth of his tribe. The cultural connection he needed would come later in life in his teenage and young adult years. He chose to follow the ways of his biological parents and his ancestors. He wanted to follow their traditions so that he could make his life richer by connecting to his cultural past.

Richard went through the Vision Quest and learned a lot while doing it. While growing up, he realized how important it was to live according to traditional values and rules. He loved the way that Ojibwe elders could connect him to his past. He studied with them so that he could learn more about the source of the world, of his people, and his place in the bigger picture of it all. As part of his learning journey, the elders helped him see he was meant to be a storyteller.

They told him that the curve of his fingers showed how well-suited he was to become a storyteller and share his journey with the world. He followed their advice and the advice of his guardian spirit. Because of this advice he published several books. And through his work as a newspaper writer, he was able to share a lot of information about the troubles facing his people and the good things that were happening within Native communities.

Richard is now a respected man who has advanced the interests of his tribe. He has shared the ways and values of the Ojibwe with other people through his writing. He made sure his tribe has a voice throughout Canada and the rest of the world. He won an award for his hard work as a writer, and many people have a high opinion of him.

The lessons Richard has taught us all is how important it is to work hard. You participate in your Vision Quest to learn what your path in life is or to confirm your decision about your life path. When you have this confirmed, you need to work towards making success on your path. It's a gift to know what you want to achieve in your life. Many people in the modern world have no idea what they want to achieve.

So take that gift and use it by putting in the effort you need towards your bright future.

Chapter Takeaways:

- Coming of age is an important part of a person's life. It's when you transform from being a child to being an adult. Once you have come of age, you are expected to act like an adult. There are rituals that are followed by most tribes when you go through this change. The rituals vary from tribe to tribe.

- Sometimes there are different rituals for boys and girls. For girls there isn't always a ritual because they go through changes in their body that clearly show they have become a woman. But, even if no rituals are done, they are still taught about their tribe, religion, and the history of the world.

- Boys normally go through rituals that involve hunting or doing things in the wilderness. Before this, they are taught what they will need to do. Just like girls, they are taught about their tribe, the Earth's history, and religious beliefs of the tribe.

- You will gain personal values when you do a coming-of-age ceremony. You will also strengthen your personal beliefs and goals.

- The Vision Quest is one of the best-known coming-of-age ceremonies. This is where the person goes into the wild to try to get a message from their spirit guide. A spirit guide is the animal or human-like animal that helps you in your life's journey. If you manage to get a message from them on your Vision Quest, they will answer questions you have and help reveal your life's path.

- The world-famous writer, Richard Wagamese, was a person who learned his life's path on his Vision Quest. He learned that his hands were the right shape and curvature to become a good writer. As such, he could focus on writing his whole life and was able to share important Native American information with the whole world.

CHAPTER 7

⌒‿‿⌒

Parents–What They Do and One Man Honoring His Mother in Ways Few Others Can

P arents in a Native American community ensure children are cared for. They make sure children become strong, independent individuals. It is important to Native people that a child is given enough independence to choose how they want to live after they become an adult. Parents take it as their responsibility to protect and guide children until they are grown enough to make those life decisions.

Parents in most Native American communities respect their children's wishes. They allow their children to see the world in their own way. The way you see the world is respected, and you're expected to respect the way others see the world. You're allowed to be creative in your own way, so long as you allow others the same right. For this reason, children are taught good manners so they understand how important it is to allow others to be themselves.

Parents often communicate with their children without using words. It's important to understand that words aren't the only way to get a message across. The way you use your hands and head (your gestures) have a big effect. Your body language shows people how you feel and how willing you are to communicate with them. The expressions on your face show when you're paying attention and how you're reacting to a situation. The way you touch a person (on their elbow, for example) shows how you feel towards them. All of these things are non-verbal ways of communicating, and all of them are used by Native American parents.

Part of the reason parents communicate non-verbally is because children aren't always expected to communicate verbally with adults. The function of a child is to learn and to become more capable. They don't yet know all the things that an adult knows. Being humble and accepting that you have a lot to learn allows you to be in the right frame of mind and get knowledge. You can't learn if you're not willing to try to learn.

Another reason why children aren't expected to talk all the time is because it allows them to see the value of silence. In the modern world we get caught up in the bustle of everything. Life seems busy, and we can't get to everything. By knowing how to be silent, we can calm our mind, body, and spirit. This helps us to face any situation. This is one of the most important skills for any child to learn. Quietness can be a very good thing.

In tribal life, it's not just the parents that raise a child. The child is raised by all the adults of the community. The adults of the community include the child's direct family, relatives, and non-family members. Elders are a particularly important group of adults when it comes to raising a child in a tribal community. The elders share the history and folklore of the tribe. This helps you gain a sense of identity as a child. You learn where your ancestors came from and how you fit into the world by listening to the stories of your elders.

As a child, you might not always live with your biological parents. In Native American communities, we pride ourselves on treating all children in our communities as if they're family, even when they're not biologically. As such, you might live with any number of people as a child. This could be your grandparents. It could be aunts or uncles. Uncles that are your mom's brothers are normally very important in your upbringing. In many cases, you might live in more than one home.

Adults in the community will often invite you into their home to feed you some of the food they've made. They look out for the children around them. This might not be safe in the big city, but in most tribes you're much safer as a child than you would be in non-tribal areas. The adults in your community often won't have any problem sharing with you or including you in their plans around the home. They might even teach you a few things while they're making you food or helping you out with homework.

One of the things you'll see when you're at the homes of the many adults in your community is the emphasis they place on personal values. As a people, Native Americans usually do not value material possessions. Rather, we value people, nature, spirituality, and the good that we can do in the world. Native people tend to share our possessions, because we want to empower those around us. Selfish members of the community are often ignored by the rest of the community, because they don't contribute to its overall state of wellness.

Generally speaking, Native people do not consider competition to be very important. We tend not to want to see our neighbors fail so that we can look better as individuals. Rather, we uplift those we deal with, even if it means we have to hide how pleased we are about something we've accomplished. We don't gloat. In this way we can help others to not feel bad about themselves. The pride we feel we keep to ourselves. It is good to work as a team. It is also good to help others reach their goals. At the same time, there's nothing wrong with being happy and proud of yourself for the hard work you've done and accomplishments you've made.

In many ways, it is good to value other people more than winning in a competition. Winning isn't everything. Valuing community and valuing other people is one of the strengths of Native American cultures. At the same time, there are downsides to not being competitive. One problem is that some children have a hard time doing well academically. Some children in Native communities are afraid that academic success may take away the spotlight from other kids. The thing is, you will be able to provide better for your community if you do well academically. You're not harming others by doing well in school. You're looking out for future generations by doing well in school. It is possible to focus on excelling in your studies while also being a good friend and neighbor to those around you. Both are possible.

Values Taught by Parents and Other Adults

Sharing is one of the most important values taught by adults. Sharing can make things a lot easier for others they're involved with. By sharing, your friends won't have to be without the things they need, and they won't get envious of you. When you share, you also create a relationship where others will help you when you need it. This will make it more pleasant to spend time around your friends.

We are also taught that interfering with others is a bad thing. Everyone has their own perspectives on how their life should be lived. They want to do things they enjoy and they want to be with people they like. We cannot live everyone else's life for them. For this reason, we are taught that noninterference is a good quality that we should try to build. Its opposite is being nosy.

Cooperation is a value that holds a lot of importance. When we work together with others in our group, more can be accomplished. Tribal communities have always prided ourselves on our ability to work with our companions. Many people outside tribal communities are taught to prioritize their own interests above the needs of others. In our communities, we're taught that working with each other can lead to better solutions than any of us would be able to achieve alone.

Focusing on the present moment is a value that helps us in our daily life. Yes, we will sometimes have to think about the future, but many people get so stuck on thinking about the future that they don't see what's right in front of them. By paying attention to what's going on in the present, we can see what problems and solutions are with us right now. We can also keep ourselves from being overwhelmed by memories. We're looking at the world around us rather than the world as it was yesterday or as it might possibly be tomorrow.

A healthy and peaceful relationship with the natural world is a value that's respected by many elders in the Native American community. All children are taught to take care of the world around them. The world around us feeds us and provides us with the things we need. It's only fair to provide some form of protection to the world as well. By taking care of Mother Nature, she is more capable of taking care of us.

Sticking with those that you owe your help and commitment to is called loyalty. It's something that can be given easily. Loyalty means supporting someone that has been there for you. Rather than getting new friends because your old friends aren't doing good, you provide your old friends with strength. By helping those that are close to you and sticking with them through the difficult times, you're building friendship groups that are based on real connections. If you have no loyalty, people may leave you, because they will feel that you are not dependable.

Respect for one's elders is also an important value for Native American adults. People that are older than you have gone through more experiences in their life. This has resulted in them being able to view life from a larger point of view. They have tried and tested many courses of actions, so they are able to give you good advice on what would be of benefit to you or what might cause you trouble. We should also remember that older people have faced a lot of difficulties in their lives, and by being kind to them and respecting them, we can make it easier for them to face their challenges.

Bill Reid

Bill Reid was a man of mixed descent. His father was of European heritage, while his mother was of Haida descent. He grew up practicing the ways of his father, because he did not know about his mother's ancestors or their customs. He only found out about his connection with the Haida tribe later when he had progressed through most of his schooling. This connection would be one of the points on which he defined his later life.

The Haida are a tribe from British Columbia in Canada. There are parts of the tribe that are also found in Alaska. The main part of the tribe is found on the group of islands called *Haida Gwaii*. The people of this tribe have a history of having strong individual villages. Their villages all have their own chiefs and are run according to the wishes of the people in that village. Each village decides for itself if it wants to remain at peace or go to war. Individual villages also decide how to deal with their resources and finances and how to celebrate their religion.

The Haida are also known for the importance they attach to ceremonies. The main type of ceremony held by the tribe is a potlatch. This is a ceremony where people give things to other people of the tribe. This helps those with lots of possessions keep the respect of those people with less possessions. It's also to assist those with political positions to remain in high regard by those they lead. Potlatches are held on many occasions, including when a member of a village builds their house or when someone wants to overcome something that has caused them embarrassment. Some of the things given at potlatches are traditional Haida art or items decorated according to Haida artistic culture.

Bill Reid was particularly affected by the art he saw when he learned more about his traditional roots. He became a jeweler and artist starting in his 2os. At first he wasn't heavily inspired by his Haida roots. But, as time passed, he became more and more connected to the artistic forms of his ancestors. He made jewelry showing myths of his culture. He also made large wooden carvings that showed scenes from its mythology.

The ways of making Haida art had been lost before he became an artist. The Canadian government had made certain rules that made it harder to practice Haida art and culture. As a result, the techniques to make traditional Haida art were lost. Bill had to look at the old art pieces that still existed and make his own techniques to continue his artistic heritage. In this way, he created new ways to make Haida art. He made it more widespread. Other people got involved, and he showed them how to make the same type of art.

With his hard work, Bill had made people all over Canada aware of the Haida culture. They loved its art and they saw its beauty. Soon, Haida art was included in important museums and other buildings. Bill made some art pieces that included many people from his mother's village. He wanted to build on his connection to her roots. To do this, he built on his link with the family and community of the village where she had come from.

The dedication of this man to his mother allowed him to build a close relationship with his tribe. As a result of the dedication, he was able to bring an ancient art form back to life. He was responsible for the Haida tribe regaining much of its sense of identity. Without his connection to his mother, none of this would have been possible. What it teaches us is that our parents can have a lasting impact on our lives. It also teaches us that we have a lot of wisdom and beauty to gain by devoting ourselves to the cultures of our ancestors. Our heritage is not something to be forgotten. It is something to be cherished and shared.

Chapter Takeaways:

- The purpose of a Native American parent is to raise a strong individual. The person is raised to be capable and independent. Their parents encourage them to achieve their goals along their own path in life.

- Parents teach their children non-verbal communication in their first few years. This helps them understand how people interact better. Non-verbal communication includes touching, body language, facial expressions, hand movements, and head movements.

- Teaching values is an important part of a parent's job. They make sure their child learns values like respecting elders, cooperation, non-interference, taking care of nature, sharing, and being in the present moment.

- Other people also do some of the things a parent would. A child might live in more than onc house while growing up. The people they live with will provide them with advice, food, and care.

- Quietness is something that is taught by parents and elders. They teach you to listen and to think about what you're listening to. In this way you actually build understanding.

- Bill Reid was a man with a Native American mom of the Haida tribe. He only found out about her connection with the tribe when he was a teenager. He became more interested in his heritage and loved the culture it represented.

- Bill Reid was a skilled artist and jeweler. He saw that the Haida ways of making art had been lost, but the way they showed art could still be protected. He took his art skill and learned how to show Haida art in new ways. Without his commitment, the Haida art system would have been lost.

- One of the reasons Bill re-formed the Haida way of making art was because he wanted to honor his mom. He grew more interested and attached to her heritage and wanted to do good for her community. He saw how using art he could bring the whole community together.

CHAPTER 8

~~~~~

Grandparents–Loving Their Grandchildren and Taking Care of the Blood of Mother Earth

Native American grandparents participate directly in raising their grandchildren. This is particularly true of grandmothers. They look after children when the mom or dad is unable to. They also look after their grandchildren to allow the mom and dad to work and gather the resources that are needed for the family. The role of a tribal grandmother has always been to make sure that her family is safe and cared for.

Older women in a tribe hold an important status. They have a position of leadership. They also give out knowledge and wisdom. The years they have been alive have given them more than enough knowledge to share with their grandchildren and other people. They also have a strong position of spiritual guidance to provide.

The presence of older women makes a village, tribe, community or reservation more stable. People know they are safe when they can go to the old women of the tribe. The old women will protect them from hunger and other problems. When you're with one of the old women of the tribe, you'll feel like you belong. They are there to nurture you and to provide you with the guidance you need to make good choices.

The values of your tribe are passed down by its older people. This is passed along through shamans and other important members of the community. Without the presence of older people, important values will be forgotten. This happened in Canada, because many people were taken away from their families and grandparents. They were no longer connected to the ways of their tribe, and they could not learn the traditions of their tribe. This was because they weren't able to communicate with the adults and older people of their communities who had knowledge about their traditions.

Grandparents are also teachers. They help children understand many important things about their communities. This includes the language of their people. Language is a way to communicate. It's also a way to strengthen the bonds of community. When someone speaks the same language as you, you feel an automatic connection. This is particularly the case when you speak a language that's not the main language of a country.

Customs are also taught by grandparents. These are the ways people do things in your community. If you don't know your customs you might offend your friends and family without even knowing it. By knowing and using your customs, you can make sure that you respect those around you.

Customs are closely linked to cultural practices. Cultural practices are also things that you're expected to do and how you're expected to do them. But, they include special activities and procedures you need to follow. They are the things that make your culture stand out from others. For example, if people of your tribe have a special dance they do every year at the start of winter, then that dance is a cultural practice. Your grandparents might also teach you spiritual beliefs and tribal history.

The function of a grandparent as a teacher allows them to make sure your culture is preserved. When they have taught you about your culture, you become a representative of it. One day you will be old and will be able to teach your grandchildren about your culture. You will become your grandchildren's advisor and mentor. They will come to you with questions and you will tell them stories about history to provide them with wisdom. The wisdom you provide them with will answer their questions and allow them to make smart decisions.

Storytelling is one of the most important activities grandparents and elders take part in. Storytelling is the glue that binds together the community. It allows older people to express their feelings about things that have happened to them and to the community. It is used to pass along the beliefs of the tribe. Folklore stories all teach morals. They let a grandparent show why specific morals are so important.

When telling a story, people who listen must keep quiet. Silence allows them to listen and think about the story being told. The listener is forced to be patient by only being allowed to ask questions after the story is finished. While patiently listening, most of the questions that would have been asked are answered in the story anyway. Further, being silent while listening makes you think deeper about the story you're hearing. It's good for the imagination.

Grandparents set an example of how to behave. You can see how they lived their lives. By seeing how they lived their lives, you can see how you might make similar or different decisions from them. They also set an example of endurance. Life can be filled with many challenges, and it may be difficult. Elders often can teach you how to face challenges that may come up. By enduring the troubles and making good decisions, you can achieve good things.

Our grandparents show us that you should be able to rely on yourself. It's okay to ask for help from other people. But, you should also understand your own abilities and make use of them. Don't ask other people to do things for you when you're perfectly capable of doing it yourself. When you break down your abilities, soon you'll start believing you're less capable than you really are. In life you need to know what your capabilities are, and you need to be confident in them. True confidence in your abilities doesn't require that you show them off to everyone. You can be confident in your abilities and be modest at the same time.

One thing that makes living a lot easier is to work in harmony with people. Avoid being confrontational. Confrontational people are always looking for a fight. When they look for a fight, they get it. If you're non-confrontational, it's easier for you to live at peace with others. This is one of the values that grandparents in the Native American community try to teach their grandchildren.

When you're able to have peaceful relations with others, you also need to accept their differences. This is called acceptance of diversity. Diversity refers to the differences between people, whether it's how they look or what groups they are a part of. Our grandparents make sure that we allow other people to have their differences. Only by allowing other people to be as they are can we expect them to allow us to be as we are.

Josephine Mandamin: The Water Matriarch

Josephine Mandamin was a grandmother who left a very big mark. She was a member of the Anishinaabe people. In her early life she was known to give back to those that needed it. She worked for many years to help students. Her job was to provide assistance to students that had trouble at home or in their life. She mainly worked with students that were mentally challenged. With her help, many of them were able to achieve their goals despite the personal challenges they faced.

Josephine was a family woman. She had five of her own children. She loved children so much that she adopted three more. She later became a grandmother and great-grandmother. She represented the Anishinaabe belief in the wisdom of their grandmothers. She was even on the Grandmothers Council.

The Grandmothers Council holds an important role. They take the wisdom of the grandmothers and make that wisdom available to members of the community. Grandmothers hold a respected position for the Anishinaabe. They have a lot of knowledge from the years they were alive. They also have experience and wisdom from decisions they have made and have seen others make.

While she was on the Grandmothers Council she taught many people things. She advised children about how to do well at home and at school. She showed young people how to decide what to do in their life. She helped young moms and dads with advice about how to raise their children. And she helped older parents with advice about how to overcome problems they faced with their children.

In the First Nations, grandmothers are holy. They are respected for the position they hold. They are often experts in their indigenous language, enabling others to remain connected with the language of their roots. They know their culture better than younger people, so can provide guidance on cultural ways. Grandmothers can also teach us how to become more confident in our identity and how we can respect the things made by the Creator.

In all her wisdom, Josephine attended one of the Sun Dance ceremonies of her nation. The ceremony was held by the Grand Chief, Eddie Bentonbenaise. At the ceremony he talked about a vision he had had. The vision showed that water would become impossible for the average person to afford. This would be because the water supplies of the world were becoming too polluted. He said this would come to pass if no one did anything about it.

Josephine took initiative. She saw the truth of the words of the Grand Chief. She wanted to leave a healthy world for her family, community, and nation. So, she took responsibility and gathered a group of volunteers. The volunteers would hold annual walks around the Great Lakes of North America. The walks were held to raise awareness of the condition of the water in the Great Lakes. People from all over Canada and the United States became aware of the problem and demanded that action be taken. Josephine and her fellow volunteers became known around the world as the Water Walkers.

The government heard the voice of the people. It felt the pressure they were putting on it to make change. Other organizations also participated in making change. The walks that Josephine and her volunteers took showed some of the main problems. This included landfill waste that was getting into the water. There were chemicals being dumped into the water. Some residents around the lakes were also using a lot more water than they needed. The Water Walkers made sure that they reported things happening that could make the water less safe to drink.

As a result of their work and the changes that were made by organizations and the government, there were many water warnings that were lifted. Water warnings can only be lifted when water becomes safe to drink again. This means that they helped make the water cleaner for everyone. For all her hard work, Josephine earned multiple awards. She also earned the name Grandmother Water Walker.

Chapter Takeaways:

- Grandparents are involved with raising their children in Native American communities. Sometimes their grandchildren will stay with them.

- A grandparent will often become a teacher for their grandchild and other people in their group. They will teach language, culture, history, customs, and religion. This is often done by telling stories.

- When a child needs advice, they can normally go to a grandparent. The grandparent will have experience, knowledge, and wisdom.

- One famous grandmother was Josephine Mandamin. She was called Grandmother Water Walker.

- When Josephine was older, she attended a Sun Dance ceremony that was held by the Grand Chief of the Anishinaabe people. He said he had a vision that water would become as expensive as gold if no one took action.

- Josephine heard the Grand Chief's message and organized a group of volunteers to do annual walks around the Great Lakes. They showed places where people were making the water polluted or where people were wasting water.

- As a result of Josephine and her volunteers' efforts, pressure was put on the government. Other organizations also hear the message. Collective action started taking place, and the drinking water supplies of the Great Lakes and other areas are much cleaner as a result.

CHAPTER 9

⌒‿⌒

Family, the Community, and One Woman Fighting Who Fought to Get Back the Rights of Her Community

F amily and the community are closely linked together. The community you live in is made up of families. Both families and communities are groups that you can rely on for support. They require your help too. In this chapter,we'll learn about at Native American family life. Then, we'll learn about Native American communities.

Family

Your family doesn't only consist of your mom, dad, brothers, and sisters. There are many other people that are a part of your family. Family includes people that are related to you by blood and people that aren't. In the Native American community we also consider people part of our family that might not be related to us. They are always involved in the family's activities and we consider them a part of our group. In many cases, we informally adopt people that we want to be a part of our family. Informal adoption brings neighbors or extended family relatives (like cousins) into our lives as if they were immediate family.

Many Nativefamilies have multiple generations of people living together. This includes grandparents, great-grandparents, and younger generations. Each generation contributes their strengths to the family unit. Older generations contribute knowledge and wisdom to the family unity. Younger generations contribute hard work and physical capabilities, and other kinds of support. There are many unrelated people that come and go out of the household, people of varying ages.

Due to this, many households have a pot of food on the stove for any person to come and eat from.

One of the reasons Native American families are so wholesome is that everyone tries to listen properly. By really listening to the people in your household, you'll really understand what they're trying to say. You'll also really understand what they're going through. With this understanding, proper connections can be built and maintained. No one feels ignored or as if they're completely unheard. They all feel as if at least one other person knows what they're going through.

Observation is also important in a Native American family. Members of the family look at those around them. They watch and listen closely to see how other family members are feeling and what they're going through. By paying attention to those around you, you can see when they need your support. You can also see when they're doing something that could have a bad effect on the family. Building observation abilities isn't only beneficial in the family environment, but in almost every environment.

By looking and listening at those around us closely, we can be better family members. The main positive result is that we'll learn to look deeper than the words people say. This is good because many people say things they don't mean. Sometimes, words alone are not enough to express what a person is going through. Sometimes people hide how they feel so that others feel better. This results in them feeling alone. By really looking at them, we can see when people are hiding how they feel. By seeing this, we can offer our support, even when they don't ask for it. They might not take our offer for help all the time, but knowing that someone cares enough to ask just might be what they need to feel better.

Community

Community holds a lot of significance for Native American groups. It's the support structure that provides a base for everyone to rely on. A community is made up of multiple families who all interact with one another. Everyone in the community knows they're a part of a group and the group is part of their identity. The community holds events together and it provides assistance to all its members. Without a community, everyone within it would be an individual struggling along to achieve their goals alone.

One of the useful things about a community is that each person has their own point of view on things. When there are problems that the community faces, having many viewpoints allows for better solutions. This is because everyone in the community can contribute their knowledge to the problem. With the problem examined from many viewpoints, it can be understood more completely.

With many perspectives comes a need to respect other people's way of seeing things. A community cannot function if everyone is shut down from mentioning their own perspective. By empowering people to share their ideas, you know you're also safer to share your own. We are all individuals, even though we're a part of the community group. We need to be uplifted as both individuals and as the community as a whole.

A perk of having a community is that you know who to go to for the things you need. You don't need to go looking for people who might be able to help you with a situation. You first go to members of your community for support before going to others. In this way, you empower them and they empower you. Only if you can't find the help you need within the community should you go out of it to look for help. Operating like this allows you to be loyal more easily.

Having a strong community helps you work through suffering more easily. If other children are bullying you, you can go to someone in your community to talk to. They can offer you advice and provide you with a tale of their experience. They can also give you advice from legends and folklore that have been told in the tribe for generations. In some cases, you might even be able to find someone in the community who will be willing to help act as a referee between you and your bully in a conversation to sort out your differences.

When you have a long-standing community, it's also easier to build up respect. Earning respect requires time. When you're in a large city where you don't know many people, the good you do won't be known by the strangers passing by. But when you're in a community, everyone knows about the good you did. They are also willing to tell people that visit the community (strangers) about your strengths when someone of your talents is needed. In this way, respect that you've worked hard to earn is recognized by all, making your life easier.

It's easier to respect the opinions of others and to not interfere with their activities when we see the good in them. One of the values that has helped us the most as Native Americans is that we see the good in people. Yes, there might be some bad in all of us. But, we choose to see the good and empower it. There is a lot of good that we can develop and share to make the world a better place. Our communities help us do exactly that.

Winona LaDuke

Winona LaDuke is a woman who has affected the lives of hundreds of thousands of people for the better. She is an activist who promotes taking care of the environment and improving the economic position of Native Americans. She has written books to highlight some of the important topics affecting the Native American community today. Her work to improve communities around the U.S. has related to land, energy production, food production, and safeguarding religious practices of native communities.

Her passion for the indigenous communities of the U.S. started young. She was born to a Russian-Jewish mom and an Ojibwe (Anishinaabe) dad. Her dad was from the White Earth Reservation in Minnesota. Although her parents divorced when she was a child and her mom wasn't of native descent, she was still encouraged to participate in indigenous activities. Her mom encouraged her to visit the White Earth Reservation. Her mom also allowed her to stay at various native communities in the summer. The result was that Winona built a very strong connection with her family origins.

She loved the way of life of native communities. She liked it to such an extent that she studied how to develop rural communities economically at Harvard. Her time at Harvard allowed her to connect with indigenous individuals from other tribes. It also allowed her to become aware of major issues that were faced by all tribes. She became passionate about making life easier for all Native Americans. She even went to the United Nations to make it known how tribal lands were being used in ways that were not sustainable and that were destructive to the land. This unsustainable use of land wasn't even being done with the purpose of benefiting tribal members.

Winona participated in other important causes on a national level while she was at Harvard and after she finished her studies. After that, she moved to the White Earth Reservation where she became a high school principal. She loved children and she loved helping those of her community reach higher levels of education. Winona's love for her community led to her getting involved in other activities that affected the reservation and her tribe.

Winona LaDuke also created a network designed to uplift indigenous women. This network gave women a bigger voice in tribal politics, religious activities, and cultural affairs. It also allowed them to participate in activities that had the purpose of getting back native land that had been taken away. With the land, members of her communities would be able to farm, to take care of natural resources, and to work towards producing sustainable energy. Her work earned her a lot of respect in the human rights profession. She was even awarded money for her hard work on human rights.

In addition, Winona started an organization that buys back tribal lands with the money she made from her human rights award. The land would be bought back for specific purposes. One of these was developing the resources of the communities she worked with in sustainable ways. Another reason was to give more economic opportunities to members of Native American citizens. With this work she got more involved in the importance of farming and good food.

Food resources are important to the whole world. When a community is in control of the food it grows and eats, as well as how this is done, it is called food sovereignty. Food sovereignty for Native American people has become one of Winona's big goals. She helped to protect local wild rice from being exploited. She also helped to establish local food systems. Farming by indigenous people with low incomes can help to uplift even poor Native Americans into a better financial position. This is one of her goals.

Winona LaDuke has shown us some very important lessons. She has shown us that it is possible to uplift indigenous communities. It's possible to do this while keeping the communities in a position where they don't have to sacrifice their cultural ways for economic benefits. They can improve their economic condition while at the same time staying true to their religious and community values. You too can make your community better.

Chapter Takeaways:

- Family is more than just your parents and your siblings. It includes your extended family like the cousins of your cousins. It also includes people that your family has adopted, even when they are adopted informally. Members of the community are frequently invited into the home and treated like family. A household will often have family members of different generations. Each generation has their own knowledge and skills to contribute to the household.

- Your community is the group of people you live in or close to. It is made up of multiple homes and families. Support is one of the main functions of a community. It provides you with some of your identity and it empowers you.

- Winona LaDuke is one person who understands why it is important to empower your community. She is from the Ojibwe tribe. She studied how to build the economies of rural areas. She formed a network of women who contribute to Native American politics, culture, and religious activities. She also formed a company that uplifts people within her communities by buying land and then lets that land be used by indigenous people in ways that can contribute to the economy. She is a good example about how one person can uplift a whole group of communities.

CHAPTER 10

~~~

Women–Their Importance in Native American Culture and Some Women Who Have Influenced the World

Women make up about half of the people on the whole planet. Without them humans would no longer be able to exist. Men cannot have children, but women can. Beyond what their bodies can do, many women also provide nurturing, love, and care that's needed by those around them. As mothers, they bring up children to become capable, strong adults.

In our communities, men often handle the hunting and protecting of the tribe. They make sure that other tribes don't hurt our own. They also make sure that we have enough food to eat and keep strong. Women, on the other hand, handle the internal activities of the tribe. The internal activities of the tribe need to be taken care of so that everyone feels comfortable and cared for.

Internal activities of the tribe include making food, making things for the house, collecting herbs and plants for food, taking care of children, and running administrative activities. Making food allows everyone to be fed so they can do their jobs. Making things for the house results in a more comfortable home life. Gathering herbs and plants takes care of medical and extra food demands. Caring for children ensures that future generations are there to take over when older generations need them to. And running administrative activities makes sure that the government of the tribe functions smoothly.

It's clear that women are capable of a lot and are essential to the functioning of our tribes. Due to their importance, women are given a lot of political, social, and economic power in Native American society. Political power includes the right to participate in choosing chiefs and other people of power in the tribe. Social power is where a woman holds influence and people come to her for advice and to be part of her social circles. Women have economic power because they often have control over the finances of a household and they have control over the resources that are kept in the home.

Matrilineal descent is where possessions and positions are passed on from mom to daughter to granddaughter. This is the way that things are passed to the next generation in Native American society. In the many non-Native societies—European societies in particular—inheritance normally takes place from dad to son to grandson (patriarchal descent). Besides material possessions, the clan you belong to is also determined by who your mom was. Part of the reason we use matrilineal descent in Native American society is because women are in charge of running home life and administering the community they live in. Since they are in charge of resources in their homes and community, it makes sense that they would pass the possessions of the house on to the next person who will do the same (either their daughter or another female relative).

Normally, women hold political power as Clan Mothers. Clan Mothers are officials within the community who hold formal authority. They can choose who will be the chief. They can also remove a chief from his position if he doesn't do what is right for the tribe. The Clan Mother is also expected to carry out the interests of her tribe. In addition to handling the important things that concern the whole tribe, the Clan Mother also helps with smaller matters. If there is an upset between members of the community or in a family and they can't work through it, the Clan Mother will make a fair decision about the upset.

The value of women goes far deeper in Native American cultures than in other cultures. In some tribes, women are given religious importance. In those tribes, the creation of the world is told to have come about because of a woman or a goddess. The goddess or woman birthed the Earth, parts of the Earth, or created the many animals, gods, and people that are part of the world. As such, it is women who are seen as the creators of this world and the people in it.

The women of the tribe are often responsible for larger amounts of the food eaten by the tribe than the men are. Men provide meat and fish by hunting and fishing. Women provide plants from gathering. This includes nuts, fruit, vegetables, and medicines. These foods are eaten as parts of a meal. They are also eaten as snacks. Without this source of food, a tribe would be restricted to meat and animal products for food.

Daily Life of a Woman in a Native American Tribe

There are some activities that are done by women in almost all tribes. Tribes do have differences, but there are some things that are common between all of them. One of these is cooking. Cooking is important to sustain the community. Women don't only cook for themselves and their own family. Many also cook enough to make sure that guests are well fed if they come by the house.

Gathering is a task that takes a lot of time. Gathering requires some knowledge. A person needs to know what plants are safe to eat and what plants are poisonous. They need to know how to tell the difference between safe plants. Harvesting the plants from the wild also requires some basic tools, otherwise the plants harvested will be damaged and the foods collected will be wilted or will get spoiled. Lessons about gathering are taught throughout a woman's childhood and during their coming-of-age ceremony training.

Tanning is a technical part of a woman's job. When men bring animals from hunts, those animals are skinned. Skinning is the job of women in most cases. It's the process of removing the skin of an animal so that the hide can be used and the meat can be used. There are specific ways to cut and remove the skin and preserve it so that it isn't damaged. If these ways are followed, the whole

Once they are skinned, women will use chemical processes to preserve the skin. By preserving the skin, it won't go rotten, but can be used. Preserving includes removing the fat under the skin, putting a lot of salt on the skin, and drying out the skin. Skins are used for things like building teepees, making clothes and shoes, making blankets, and more.

Teepees are also the responsibility of women. Teepees are the homes of many Native American tribes. They are mainly made for temporary purposes, such as moving the tribe around during hunting season. They are used for important events, such as the coming-of-age ceremonies of girls. Sometimes teepees are used as homes, especially in tribes where a lot of moving around happens. In a few cases a teepee is used as a permanent home.

To make a teepee a woman needs wooden poles and animal hides. She will make a framework from the poles. Then, she'll put animal hides over this framework. The wooden frame keeps the structure strong, while the hides keep the people inside safe from the weather. Maintenance is important once the teepees have been constructed, which is also the job of women.

During their time off, many Native American women play sports and games. The most popular sport is probably shinny. Shinny is a game where a ball is hit with sticks. The purpose of this is to get the ball in the goals of the other team. The ball can be made of different materials, but is normally made from leather that's stitched together tightly. The sticks can vary in shape and often have a curve at the bottom (almost in the shape of a hockey stick). And the goals are made by putting two sticks in the ground on each side of the shinny pitch.

Shinny is a game that has been part of Native American tradition for hundreds of years. There are myths and folktales that include the sport. This game is good for all tribes to play, because it can be played on the ground or on ice or on icy ground. When it's played on ice, it's played without using scates. When playing the game, the stick and the feet may both be used to move the ball. The rules vary from tribe to tribe, but the basic point remains to get the ball into the opposing team's goals by hitting it with the stick. It's a good game to build teamwork and team spirit.

Katteuha

During its formation, the form of government that would be used in the United States was up for debate. There were many opinions about how it should be formed. There were people fighting for the US government to form in a way that served their interests. The Founding Fathers listened to many of these opinions and points of view. They also observed the governments of other countries and of the Native American tribes. The Iroquois nations were of particular interest.

Benjamin Franklin was the Founding Father who most openly showed interest in the Native American form of government. He noted that it was a humane form of government. There were no prisons. There were also no institutions to inflict punishment and to force compliance with the rules. It was clear that Native Americans respected independence and freedom. Their administration worked to instill ethics and accountability so that people took responsibility for their own conduct. As such, there was less of a need for everyone else in the tribe to force someone to not do wrong.

Most white people at the time looked down on Native Americans as "noble savages" (Gilio-Whitaker, 2019). Despite this, Native people played a big part in influencing the Articles of Confederation. The Articles formed the United States into a confederation. As such, all the states party to it had a part to play in running the national government. There were many similarities with the Iroquois form of administration because the Iroquois also considered the votes and opinions of all members in running the tribe and nations.

Despite the strong influence the Native Americans had on the first government of the United States, they were still looked down upon by many colonists. They were seen as less sophisticated. Native people were seen as undeveloped because of their connection to nature. In reality, Natives' bond with nature helped them to create a way to preserve natural resources. The colonists failed to realize how truly sophisticated the Native American way of life really was. They made trouble for the Native Americans because of their low opinion of them.

There were some Native American women who were able to make a lot of positive changes in spite of the negative point of view colonists had about them. Katteuha was one example of this. She wrote a letter to Benjamin Franklin so that he would consider Native American points of view for the Constitutional Convention. The Constitutional Convention was the event where the Articles of Confederation were examined and debated before forming the Constitution of the United States.

Katteuha was one of the most prominent Native Americans of her time. She held the position of *ghighau*. Translated, this means "beloved woman." She was the most senior woman in the Cherokee nation. Her influence included power over money and resources of the Cherokee. It also included the right to run meetings and to act as the Ambassador of the Cherokee in relation to other nations and tribes.

What we do know is that Ketteuha was the representative of the entire Cherokee nation. Her letter was read by President Benjamin Franklin. Her letter was meant to be considered by Franklin and communicated by him to the other delegates of the Constitutional Convention. Like many people of European descent at the time, Franklin thought women were inferior to men. The Native Americans were more sophisticated in that they respected the position of women in the world. They saw women as sources of true wisdom.

In her letter to the president, Ketteuha was direct. She was clear with what she meant, and she used her status as a woman as a strength rather than a weakness. She stated that because she was a woman she could have children. As a woman capable of creating life, she had the right to be heard. She would not be ignored and she would not be limited in her powers because of her sex. The confidence in her letter inspired many other women, both Native American and others. It inspired other women to stand up for their communities and themselves. Those women petitioned, sent letters, and gave speeches with the purpose of improving life for all Native American tribes.

Chapter Takeaways:

- Women hold the key to life. They can give birth and they can care for children as they grow up.

- Women have multiple important roles in their villages. This includes making leather, gathering food, collecting medicinal plants, making food, building and taking care of teepees or houses, governing the community, and participating in administration of tribal activities involving more than just one village.

- Possessions and positions are passed along with matrilineal descent in nearly all Native American tribes.

- The Clan Mother is a woman who holds an important governing position in her nation. She may help choose chiefs and get rid of chiefs. She needs to act in the best interests of her people. In many cases she helps to resolve conflicts between people within her communities.

- Ketteuha was a representative of the Cherokee nation at the time of the drafting of the Constitution of the United States. She wrote a letter to Benjamin Franklin advocating for the rights of her people. She told him that he's not allowed to treat her as less because she is a woman. Her status as a woman was something that should have been a cause for respect.

CHAPTER II

~⌒~⌒~

Mother Earth and Those That Support Her

Mother Earth is a figure of religious significance. She is central to the religious teachings of cultures from around the world. The Native American nations and the First Nations tribes in Canada also include her in many of their religions. There are differences in the myths about her from tribe to tribe, but some parts of the myth stay the same for the majority of the groups. Nearly all of these groups include Mother Earth as part of their creation story. A creation story is the myth of a culture about how the world began.

There are other figures in the creation stories of the Native American peoples. That said, Mother Earth is the one who is credited with the creation of life. She is variously described as the original woman and as a goddess. In some stories she is the only creation figure. In other stories she is one of multiple creation figures. But, she consistently is described as the originator of life and is believed to currently sustain all life on Earth.

We will look at the creation story of the Anishnaabe for a description of Mother Earth. The Anishnaabe are a group of nations and tribes who are part of Canada's First Nations. They share a common history and they have a common language. The Ojibwe are included in the Anishnaabe. This group of nations is known for its music, art, and singing traditions.

The story of creation says that there was a divine family before the start of time. This family had a grandfather. The grandfather was the Sun. There was a grandmother, who was the Moon. There was the mother, who was the Earth. And there was the Creator. The mother is who we refer to as Mother Earth.

The creator saw that the Earth was without life. It was just sand and dirt. The Creator envisioned more for the Earth. It sent down seeds of life to the fertile ground of the Earth. These seeds were carried down by birds from the Spirit World. The blood of Mother Earth was the water of the world. The water gave life to the seeds that had been brought down.

With the seeds given life and a place to grow, Mother Earth became a holder of living things. She held the plants of the world. The flowers of the world grew upon her. And the forests of the planet rested on her. By being a provider of life, she gave power to the vision of the Creator. Once the plants of the world were plentiful, the Creator sent more living creatures to Mother Earth.

The living creatures included fish. The fish filled the seas, rivers, and lakes. Land animals were sent to run and live across Mother Earth. Insects were sent from the Creator along with the fish and animals. With the arrival of the animals, fish, and insects, the world was abundant with living things. The Creator was ready to put their own image upon the world.

The Creator made the first man in their own image. The first man would have similarities to the Creator. All four elements were included in the first man. The elements were wind, earth, water, and fire. A breath of the creator was included with the four elements. The breath would give humanity its soul. Once the original man was brought into existence, the Creator let him down onto Mother Earth. This was the first man that all of us humans come from.

In the creation story above, you can see that without Mother Earth none of the rest would have been possible. She gives life with her blood–her blood being water. She also provided the resting ground for all the plants and other living creatures to rest on and run across. Mother Earth still sustains us all. Without her life would not be possible and we would not be here. This is the reason Native Americans have so much respect for her and treat life on Earth as holy.

Chief Tecumseh

Chief Tecumseh was a famous warrior. He was a Shawnee chief. The Shawnees were a strong nation that defended themselves against the efforts of Europeans to colonize them. Despite this, they were under threat from the activities of William Henry Harrison. Harrison was the Governor of the Indiana Territory at the time (the early 1800s). While he was governor, he ruled tough and he allowed little pursuit of happiness for the Native Americans in and around his territory.

Harrison was the Superintendent for Indian Affairs in the American Northwest at the time as well. This meant that he was in charge of all Native American people and their activities in the Northwest of the US. As such, he could exert a lot of pressure onto the Native Americans. Nowhere was this clearer than when it came to land. He pushed the Native Americans to give away their land, despite a treaty that had already been signed to allow them control and access of their land.

He made Native Americans give away their land so that it could be sold to white settlers. This made a lot of money for those connected with Harrison at the time. But, it did not make much money for the Native Americans involved. Chief Tecumseh was not happy with this situation that Harrison had created. He wanted to change it so that land would no longer be taken away.

Tecumseh believed that land belonged to the Shawnee chief god, who's called the Master of Life. He believed that the land should be available to all Native Americans, even those that weren't from his own tribe. He enlisted help from his brother to try to fight for the land rights of the Shawnee and other tribes. His brother was an influential individual who was called the Prophet. People believed that his brother could communicate directly with the Master of Life.

His brother was able to use his reputation to get many people to agree to join Tecumseh's cause. Tecumseh's cause was to form a confederation of Native American tribes. What was remarkable about Tecumseh's efforts was that he even united tribes that didn't normally get along. The tribes would then work together to get rid of any negative influence from colonists and settlers. This would require rejecting their ways and items. Some tribes and villages were willing to join the cause, while others weren't. Those that weren't had either formed agreements with the settlers or started enjoying the tools and ways of life of the settlers.

Tecumseh managed to bring together a large group of followers. He gave them tools, food, and supplies where he could. However, he didn't have enough–particularly when it came to weapons. He tried to gather more members for his confederation and more supplies. While in the south of the US, his brother decided to attack William Henry Harrison and the army that was close to the largest Shawnee town. They didn't have enough weapons and weren't strong enough as a group yet. As a result Harrison defeated them and destroyed the town.

After the defeat, very few tribes and villages were willing to continue supporting Tecumseh's cause. They felt that it would lead to defeat once more. Tecumseh didn't give up on his cause. He kept working towards success until he was defeated in another battle against the United States military. Despite his defeat and despite the confederation not being a success, Tecumseh left a mark. He is one of the most well-known Native Americans in history. He was a man of integrity and he pursued goals that he believed were just. He stood by his beliefs and morals.

One of the beliefs that Tecumseh held near his heart was the support of Mother Earth and all her creations. One of his most famous quotes is "The earth is my mother, and on her bosom I shall repose." This means that he would rest on the earth knowing that Mother Earth was looking out for him, protecting him, and providing. He held deep respect for Mother Earth and verbally defended her sacred power to many. He repeated many times that Mother Earth was the lifegiver. As one of the most influential Native Americans in history, his outspoken support of taking care of the Earth still sets an example to people today.

Chief Seattle

Chief Seattle (also known as Sealth) was of the Suquamish and Duwamish tribes. He was one of their tribal leaders. These two tribes didn't make a person a chief because of their birth. They made someone a chief or leader if that person was capable. Chief Seattle was both a capable speaker and a capable leader. He was able to encourage a more peaceful transition from a fully indigenous lifestyle to one that mixed Native and European practices. Earlier chiefs had not been as successful. Seattle did this by working with settlers to ensure peace for the Suquamish and Duwamish tribes.

One of the settlers he worked with frequently was Doctor David Swinson Maynard. He was a medical doctor who had moved to the Seattle area and became a general trader. He ran multiple businesses and participated in numerous activities for profit. He promoted business participation in the area, including actively looking for ways to convince people of different talents to come to the area. He had good relations with the Native Americans of the area, being particularly good friends with Chief Seattle. During his relations with the Native Americans he worked with, Maynard provided medical services and helped advance their interests in the town.

The town had originally been called Duwamp. Duwamp was a village when Doctor Maynard arrived. He was the one that suggested the name of the settlement be changed to Seattle. This was in honor of Chief Seattle. Chief Seattle was known to foster good relations with the settlers. He encouraged trade between the settlers and his people. The town became a flourishing community and grew with participation from both groups. The main trouble at the time came from unhappiness among some Native Americans who had been given bad land deals by the governor of the Washington Territory, Isaac Stevens, in treaties that had taken place under his authority.

Isaac Stevens was a person of passion. He liked to fight. He had received military training and had participated in army activities throughout his life. While Stevens was governor of Washington Territory, he also held the position of the Superintendent of Indian Affairs. He had a lot of control on the way the government managed its relationship with Native Americans because of this. It was in his interests and the interests of others he associated with to get Native American land and use it for other financial activities. He actively participated in moving Native Americans into reservations.

The treaties that took place under the Stevens' office made it difficult for many Native Americans to survive. They had less access to land, and they didn't have access to the same resources. As such, they were angry with the settlers and they needed to take supplies from settlers to survive. The town of Seattle was one of the areas that was attacked to get supplies. This took place at the Battle of Seattle.

Chief Seattle warned those living in the town of the attack. He warned both Native Americans and settlers living in the town. The town itself had a harmonious environment where all its folk could survive. With his warning and other steps that had been taken by the people in the settlement, the battle only lasted a day. Those that had come into the town to take supplies had gotten what they needed and most of the people from the town had remained safe.

Once the battle was over, Chief Seattle assisted in making sure the town would be safe from future attacks. He also continued on his quest to make sure his people, the Duwamish and the Suquamish, were able to coexist with the town's inhabitants. He knew why those that had come into the town to take supplies had done what they had done. He was a man of great character and he focused on building up his community rather than seeking to retaliate against those that had participated in the battle.

The many examples of bravery and wisdom made him one of the most respected Native American chiefs. People still refer to his actions today. As part of the legacy he left, he made sure the world understood how important the land and Mother Earth were to his tribes. He stated that the soil had witnessed what had happened to Native Americans throughout history. The land knew Native American feet and loved them for having taken good care of it. It understood how they had suffered as a nation and it was the connection between the lives of all of them, both those that were alive and those that were not.

Chief Seattle did not believe that land could be owned by private individuals. The land was part of the world in the same way as the sky and the sun. He stated that the sky and sun could not be owned—so why could the land? He further stated that the Earth was the mother of the Native American people, and she took care of them. He knew that the settlers would take land, so his request was that they would take care of it in the same way as the Native Americans had.

Chapter Takeaways:

- Mother Earth is a religious figure. In many Native American creation stories, the Creator seeded Mother Earth, allowing plants to grow on her. The creator also sent down fish, animals, insects, and the original men to populate her.

- The water of the world is her blood. Her blood sustains all upon her. She is the growing, protecting, nurturing force of the world.

- Chief Tecumseh was a Shawnee chief. He brought together people of many tribes to protect their land from being taken away and to protect Native American traditional ways of life. Those that joined him were defeated while he was away. After the defeat, very few would join him to continue pursuing his purpose. Despite the failure, he was able to bring together tribes that had clashed for years. He showed that the tribes can work together and he did this by getting him to help defend the land and to honor Mother Earth. He wanted the land to be respected and to be used in ways that would not damage Mother Earth.

- Chief Seattle was a chief of the Duwamish and Suquamish tribes. The city of Seattle was named after him. With the help of Doctor David Swinson Maynard, he was able to establish a peaceful town of Native Americans and settlers. He helped defend both indigenous people and settlers when invaders came to the town by giving them a warning about battle to come. He is one of the most famous Native American chiefs of all time. He believed that Mother Earth has a special connection to Native Americans because she has known them for many generations and has seen their suffering. He asked settlers to respect Mother Earth as the Native Americans had.

CONCLUSION

N ative Americans are a strong people. We have had many great leaders through the ages. Our leaders have shown us how to be wise and how to make the world a better place. With their examples, we have seen that peace is how to keep the world from becoming a worse place. By loving other people and working with them, we can achieve bigger things.

One of the things we looked at was being born and growing up. This is one of the most important parts of your life. When you are born you become a part of your community. They welcome you and perform rituals to make sure you will grow up to be healthy. Your mom will be taught what to do to make your birth as good as possible. Once you are born, she will keep you close so that you can remain safe while she works.

As you grow up, you start observing your parents. You look at what they do so that you can understand their jobs. You try to copy them so that you can learn their skills. When a boy is with his father he will learn how to do things like hunt and fight. When a girl is with her mother, she will learn how to do things like gather food, manage the house, or participate in governing the town or village.

As you grow older, you get ready to become an adult. At this point, you might do a coming-of-age ceremony. The ceremony will teach you about things that you need to know as an adult. This includes how the world came to be, what the history of your town is, and the beliefs of your community. You might need to go into nature by yourself to reach your spirit guide and ask them for assistance in answering your questions or finding your path in life. Once you have completed your coming-of-age rituals, you are expected to act like an adult.

As an adult you might become a parent. Your responsibility is to care for your children. While caring for them, you should take steps to show them they are in control of their own future. By raising them to be capable, they will become strong individuals that can independently take control of their future.

Grandparents, other family members, and the community will also play a role in raising a child. They look out for you as a child, even when they're not directly related to you. If you need guidance, you can go to them. Whatever their age, there is some knowledge or skill they can share with you. Native American communities are fortunate to incorporate the care of children into their identity as a community.

Women are the creators of life. They can make children and they can raise children. They carry the holy water inside of them that has been passed down to them from Mother Earth. Mother Earth has given life to all with her life force. She passes on her life force in the form of the living water of Earth. By respecting our Mother Earth and caring for her, she can return that care and provide life for future generations.

Native American culture differs from tribe to tribe. There are so many differences, yet there are so many similarities. The way of life of the indigenous people of North America is sacred and should be respected. We need to regard the way of life of the Native American people as something to be proud of and to share with the world.

References

A Day in the Life of Native Indian Americans. (n.d.). The People's Paths Resource. https://www.yvwiiusdinvnohii.net/a-day-in-the-life-of-native-indian-americans/

About the Delaware Tribal Seal. (n.d.). Official Website of the Delaware Tribe of Indians. Retrieved October 15, 2022, from https://delawaretribe.org/home-page/about-our-tribal-seal/

American Indian Women. (n.d.). Teaching History. https://teachinghistory.org/history-content/ask-a-historian/23931#:~:text=They%20usually%20owned%20the%20family

Apache Creation. (n.d.). University of California, Santa Barbara. Retrieved October 19, 2022, from https://archserve.id.ucsb.edu/courses/rs/natlink/apache/apa_creation.htm#:~:text=The%20Mescalero%20Apache%20creation%20story

Apache: Creation Story. (n.d.). The Office. https://the-office.com/bedtime-story/apache-creation.htm

Bailey, S. J., Letiecq, B. L., Visconti, K., & Tucker, N. (2019). Rural Native and European American custodial grandparents: Stressors, resources, and resilience. *Journal of Cross-Cultural Gerontology*, 34(2), 131–148. https://doi.org/10.1007/s10823-019-09372-w

Baker, J., & Coumans, H. (2020, February 6). *Home in Lenapehoking*. Urban Omnibus. https://urbanomnibus.net/2020/02/home-in-lenapehoking/

Baker, M. (n.d.). *Unami (Delaware / Lenni-Lenape) (North American tribes)*. The History Files. https://www.historyfiles.co.uk/KingListsAmericas/NorthDelawareUnami.htm

Barbour, H. (2021, November 25). *200+ famous Native Americans [Chiefs, celebs, models, politicians, actors, musicians & more!]*. Ongig. https://blog.ongig.com/diversity-and-inclusion/famous-native-americans/

Barthet, R. (2021, July 21). *St. Tammany Day is May 1*. Tammany Family. https://tammanyfamily.blogspot.com/2021/07/st-tammany-day-is-may-1.html

Benton-Banai, E. (2010). *The Mishomis Book: The Voice of the Ojibway*. University Of Minnesota Press ; Hayward, Wi.

Biographies of Plains Indians: Dull Knife - 1810-1883. (n.d.). Northern Plains Reservation Aid. http://www.nativepartnership.org/site/PageServer?pagename=airc_bio_dullknife

Brief history. (n.d.). Mohican.com. https://www.mohican.com/brief-history/

Byers, L. (2010). Native American Grandmothers: Cultural Tradition and Contemporary Necessity. *Journal of Ethnic and Cultural Diversity in Social Work*, 19(4), 305–316. https://doi.org/10.1080/15313204.2010.523653

Cave, K., & McKay, S. (2016, December 12). *Water Song: Indigenous Women and Water*. Resilience. https://www.resilience.org/stories/2016-12-12/water-song-indigenous-women-and-water/#:~:text=Indigenous%20women%20have%20a%20strong

Chief Seattle. (n.d.). New World Encyclopedia. https://www.newworldencyclopedia.org/entry/Chief_Seattle

Chief Seattle. (1854). *"Earth is our mother" [Speech transcript]*. chrome-extension://efaidnbmnnnibpcajpcglclefindmkaj/https://www.novachorus.org/archives/spr17/2017-0225_Earth_is_our_mother.pdf

Clan Mothers. (n.d.). Onondaga Nation.
https://www.onondaganation.org/government/clan-mothers/

Clan System. (n.d.). Nanticoke Lenni-Lenape Tribal Nation.
https://nlltribe.com/clan-system/

Coming of Age. (2022, June 28). Hudson County Community
College: College Libraries.
https://library.hccc.edu/c.php?g=931124&p=6713635

Confederation vs Federation. (n.d.). Diffen.
https://www.diffen.com/difference/Confederation_vs_Federation#:~:t
ext=In%20a%20Confederation%2C%20the%20federal

Constitutional Convention and Ratification, 1787–1789. (n.d.). Office
of the Historian. https://history.state.gov/milestones/1784-
1800/convention-and-
ratification#:~:text=The%20Constitutional%20Convention%20in%
20Philadelphia

Crowley, W., & Wilma, D. (2003, February 15). *Native Americans
attack Seattle on January 26, 1856*. History Link.
https://www.historylink.org/File/5208

Definition of Mohawk. (n.d.). Merriam-Webster.
https://www.merriam-webster.com/dictionary/Mohawk

Dr. Susan La Flesche Picotte. (n.d.). Changing the Face of Medicine.
https://cfmedicine.nlm.nih.gov/physicians/biography_253.html

Eastman, C. A. (1918). *Dull Knife – Northern Cheyenne Chief*.
Legends of America.
https://www.google.com/url?q=https://www.legendsofamerica.com/n
a-
dullknife/&sa=D&source=docs&ust=1666892331241932&usg=AOv
Vaw29axE9wVKt10C1XH8hIOGp

Family Values, Hierarchies and Beliefs. (n.d.). Menominee Indian Tribe of Wisconsin. https://sites.google.com/site/thecultureofnativeamericans/family-values-hierarchys-and-beliefs

Gallant, D. J. (2020, December 2). *Josephine Mandamin.* The Canadian Encyclopedia. https://www.thecanadianencyclopedia.ca/en/article/josephine-mandamin

Gilio-Whitaker, D. (2019, February 27). *Native American Influence on the Founding of the U.S.* Thought Co. https://www.thoughtco.com/native-american-influence-on-founding-fathers-2477984#:~:text=Benjamin%20Franklin

Gill, S. (n.d.). *Mother Earth: An American Story.* Religious Studies: College of Arts and Sciences; University of Colorado Boulder. https://www.colorado.edu/rlst/mother-earth-american-story

Grandmother Josephine Mandamin. (n.d.). City of Thunder Bay. https://www.thunderbay.ca/en/city-hall/grandmother-josephine-mandamin.aspx

Grandmothers Council. (n.d.). Assembly of Manitoba Chiefs. Retrieved October 26, 2022, from https://manitobachiefs.com/policy-sectors/grandmothers-council/

Group of Native American chiefs. (n.d.). University of Michigan Library. https://apps.lib.umich.edu/online-exhibits/exhibits/show/great-native-american-chiefs/group-of-native-american-chief

Harper, M. (2018, May 29). *On the Shores of the "Great Water": The Ojibwe People's Migration to Gichigamiing.* The Growler. https://growlermag.com/on-the-shores-of-the-great-water-the-ojibwe-peoples-migration-to-gichigamiing/

Hau Koda - Hello friend...Welcome to Crow Creek connections. (n.d.). Crow Creek Connections. http://www.crowcreekconnections.org/

Hazard, S., Linn, J. B., Egle, W. H., Reed, G. E., Montgomery, T. L., MacKinney, G., & Hoban, C. F. (1855). *Pennsylvania Archives.* In Google Books. J. Severns & Company. http://www.google.it.ao/books?pg=PA181&dq=editions:ISBN08039 74612&lr=&id=1HYOAAAAYAAJ&output=html_text

Hele, K. S. (2022, October 19). *Anishinaabe.* The Canadian Encyclopedia. https://www.thecanadianencyclopedia.ca/en/article/anishinaabe

History.com Editors. (2022, September 21). *Tecumseh.* History; A&E Television Networks. https://www.history.com/topics/native-american-history/tecumseh

Honouring Water. (n.d.). Assembly of First Nations. https://www.google.com/url?q=https://www.afn.ca/honoring-water/&sa=D&source=docs&ust=1666892164397221&usg=AOvVa w0TqVKasIphHqVlcTK2JNOv

How Native American Women Gave Birth. (n.d.). Sherman Indian Museum. http://www.shermanindianmuseum.org/how-native-american-women-gave-birth.html#:~:text=Women%20were%20giving%20birth%20standin g

Hoxie, F. E. (2013). Four American Indian Heroes You've Never Heard Of. *Magazine of the Smithsonian's National Museum of the American Indian*, Vol 14, No 1. https://www.google.com/url?q=https://www.americanindianmagazine .org/story/four-american-indian-heroes-youve-never-heard&sa=D&source=docs&ust=1666693800811385&usg=AOvVa w0L25D_ijHAOvOaaVy27W-a

In Memoriam: Bill Reid (1920-1998). (n.d.). Canadian Museum of History. https://www.historymuseum.ca/cmc/exhibitions/aborig/reid/reid02e.html

Indiana Territory. (n.d.). Ohio History Central. https://ohiohistorycentral.org/w/Indiana_Territory

Indigenous Peoples and Communities. (2022, August 30). Government of Canada. https://www.rcaanc-cirnac.gc.ca/eng/1100100013785/1529102490303

Jabr, F. (2013, June 3). *How to Really Eat Like a Hunter-Gatherer: Why the Paleo Diet Is Half-baked [Interactive & infographic].* Scientific American. https://www.scientificamerican.com/article/why-paleo-diet-half-baked-how-hunter-gatherer-really-eat/

Josephine Mandamin: Sacred Water Walkers - Watershed Ways. (2019, September). Art and Education. https://www.artandeducation.net/classroom/video/288709/josephine-mandamin-sacred-water-walkers

Koithan, M., & Farrell, C. (2010). Indigenous Native American Healing Traditions. *The Journal for Nurse Practitioners*, 6(6), 477–478. https://doi.org/10.1016/j.nurpra.2010.03.016

Licht, W., Lloyd, M. F., Duffin, J. M., & McConaghy, M. D. (n.d.). *The Original People and Their Land: The Lenape, Pre-History to the 18th Century.* West Philadelphia Collaborative History. https://collaborativehistory.gse.upenn.edu/stories/original-people-and-their-land-lenape-pre-history-18th-century

Lost in Time: Chief Tamanend. (2015, May 4). Bucks County Courier Times. https://www.buckscountycouriertimes.com/story/lifestyle/columns/2015/05/04/lost-in-time-chief-tamanend/18075729007/

Lundin, J. W., & Lundin, S. J. (2012, November 9). *Idaho: When It Was Part of Washington*. History Link. https://www.historylink.org/File/10237

Mallory at Tribal Trade. (2020). *Creation Story (The Mother Earth Creation Story - Indigenous Teaching)* [Video]. In YouTube. https://www.youtube.com/watch?v=HPhKHODHfFc

McDermott. (2001). *Chapter 4 - Parenting and Ethnicity* in The Handbook of Diversity in Parent Education: The Changing Faces of Parenting and Parent Education (pp. 73–96). Academic Press. https://www.sciencedirect.com/science/article/pii/B97801225648335 00058

McIntosh, E. (2020, January 24). *What we mean when we say Indigenous land is "unceded."* Canada's National Observer. https://www.nationalobserver.com/2020/01/24/analysis/what-we-mean-when-we-say-indigenous-land-unceded

McMaster, G. (2020, December 23). *By reconnecting with his Haida roots, Bill Reid catalyzed a cultural reclamation that continues today*. CBC. https://www.cbc.ca/arts/by-reconnecting-with-his-haida-roots-bill-reid-catalyzed-a-cultural-reclamation-that-continues-today-1.5850911

Montiel, A., & Cohen, S. (2020, November 2). *Twelve women to know for national Native American heritage month*. Smithsonian. https://womenshistory.si.edu/stories/twelve-women-know-national-native-american-heritage-month

Moulder, M. A. (n.d.). *"[T]hey ought to mind what a woman says": Early Cherokee Women's Rhetorical Traditions and Rhetorical Education* [Doctorate dissertation]. chrome-extension://efaidnbmnnnibpcajpcglclefindmkaj/https://repositories.lib.utexas.edu/bitstream/handle/2152/ETD-UT-2010-08-1579/MOULDER-DISSERTATION.pdf?sequence=1&isAllowed=y

Mühl, J. (2009). A Quest for Native American Identity: The Roles of Fathers and Mentors in the Works of Richard Wagamese [Master's thesis, University of Graz]. chrome-extension://efaidnbmnnnibpcajpcglclefindmkaj/https://unipub.uni-graz.at/obvugrhs/download/pdf/207225?originalFilename=true

Mustful, C. (2018, September 18). *Resisting Removal: Chief Buffalo (Kechewaishke)*. Colin Mustful: History Through Fiction. https://www.google.com/url?q=https://www.colinmustful.com/resisting-removal-chief-buffalo-kechewaishke/&sa=D&source=docs&ust=1666891280359508&usg=AOvVaw04C_tL_-PANMTBcHecQNtM

Muza, S. (2014, November 17). *Series: Welcoming All Families: Supporting the Native American Family*. Lamaze International. https://www.lamaze.org/Connecting-the-Dots/series-welcoming-all-families-supporting-the-native-american-family#:~:text=Native%20Americans%20were%20known%20to%20give%20birth%20in%20a%20simple

Mvskoke (Muscogee). (n.d.). Native Land Digital. https://native-land.ca/maps-old/territories/muscogee/

Nagy, C. (2022, October 5). *14 Indigenous Heroes Every Kid Should Know About*. Tinybeans. https://tinybeans.com/indigenous-people-your-kids-should-know/slide/1

Nathan, A. (2021, March 23). *Susan La Flesche Picotte: Leader in Tribal Health With Eye Toward Sovereignty*. Science in the News; Harvard University: The Graduate School of Arts and Sciences. https://sitn.hms.harvard.edu/flash/2021/susan-la-flesche-picotte-leader-in-tribal-health-with-eye-toward-sovereignty/

Native American Cultures. (2021, November 2). History. https://www.history.com/topics/native-american-history/native-american-cultures

Native American Oral Traditions. (n.d.). Dominican University. https://research.dom.edu/NativeAmericanStudies/myth

Native American Shinny (hockey). (n.d.). Health Ahoy. https://healthahoy.com/ancient-sports/native-american-shinny-hockey/

Native Americans: Agriculture and Food. (n.d.). Ducksters. https://www.ducksters.com/history/native_american_agriculture_foo d.php#:~:text=Gathering%20is%20when%20people%20get

Native Americans: Famous Native Americans. (n.d.). Ducksters. https://www.ducksters.com/history/famous_native_americans.php

Native connection to Unci Maka–Mother Earth. (2022, April 21). Native Hope. https://blog.nativehope.org/we-are-the-land

Nelson, D., Silva, N., & McKee, J. (2010, September 6). *Four Days, Nights: A Girls' Coming-of-Age Ceremony.* National Public Radio. https://www.npr.org/2010/09/06/129611281/four-days-nights-a-girls-coming-of-age-ceremony

North, J. (2020, July 27). *Exiled to Indian Country: Osage Nation.* Gaylord News. https://gaylordnews.net/6121/culture/osage-land/

Office of Indian Education. (n.d.). American Indian history, culture, and language: Curriculum framework: Family life. Minnesota Department of Education.

Ojibwe. (n.d.). Multilingualism and Education in Wisconsin. https://www.teachlangwisconsin.com/ojibwe

Ondich, J. L. (n.d.). *History, Beliefs, Rituals, Legends.* Minnesota Libraries Publishing Project. https://mlpp.pressbooks.pub/worldreligionsthespiritsearching/chapter /mythology-folklore-legends/

Ott, T. (2020, November 4). *12 Influential Native American Leaders.* Biography. https://www.biography.com/news/influential-native-americans-list

Pauls, E. P. (2018). *Tepee: Dwelling.* In Encyclopædia Britannica. https://www.britannica.com/technology/tepee

Pauls, E. P. (2019). *Mohican.* In Encyclopædia Britannica. https://www.britannica.com/topic/Mohican

Pauls, E. P. (2022, January 1). *The Prophet: Shawnee leader.* Encyclopedia Britannica. https://www.britannica.com/biography/The-Prophet-Shawnee-leader

Perry, A. (2020, May 5). *The place they will be born: Mohawk Midwives and Mothers.* Imperial Medicine Blog; Imperial College London. https://blogs.imperial.ac.uk/imperial-medicine/2020/05/05/the-place-they-will-be-born-mohawk-midwives-and-mothers/

Richards, K. (2022, April 28). *Isaac Ingalls Stevens (1818-1862).* Oregon Encyclopedia. https://www.oregonencyclopedia.org/articles/stevens_isaac_ingalls/#.Y1eHsOxBxQI

Rites of Passage Council. (2019a). *What is "The Calling?"* [Video]. In YouTube. https://www.youtube.com/watch?v=KOZEMIabMB4&t=52s

Rites of Passage Council. (2019b). *Vision Quest Ceremony: From Misfit to Belonging* [Video]. In YouTube. https://www.youtube.com/watch?v=H7wXW1pQSlA&t=2s

Rochester, J. (1998, November 10). *Maynard, Dr. David Swinson (1808-1873).* History Link. https://www.historylink.org/file/315

Rotinonhsyonni – Haudenosaunee (Iroquois) Confederacy. (n.d.). MBQ. https://mbq-tmt.org/mohawk-culture/

Rybak, C., & Decker-Fitts, A. (2009). Theory and Practice: Understanding Native American Healing Practices. *Counseling Psychology Quarterly*, 22(3), 333–342. Routledge. chrome-extension://efaidnbmnnnibpcajpcglclefindmkaj/https://my.enmu.edu/c/document_library/get_file?uuid=50927632-e6c2-4470-86af-ea34dc5ea5d1&groupId=4153058&filename=sbrybak-nur417.pdf

Silvey, L. A. E., Bailey, S. J., & Ponzetti, Jr., J. J. (2019). Understanding the Role of Grandparents in Indigenous Families: Principles for Engagement. *Family Science Review*, 23(2). https://doi.org/10.26536/pjvq7990

Skyhawk, S. (2018, September 13). Why do tribes have matrilineal societies? Sonny Skyhawk addresses the tradition of matrilineal governance of Native American societies. Indian Country Today. https://indiancountrytoday.com/archive/why-do-tribes-have-matrilineal-societies

Sports from around the world (North America). (2019, April 27). Montessori Physical Education. https://www.montessoriphysicaleducation.com/new-blog/native-american-sports-shinny-lacrosse-and-stickball2019/4/24#:~:text=Native%20Americans%20played%20a%20form

Stone, A. B. (2021, July 22). *Treaty of La Pointe, 1854*. MNOpedia. https://www.mnopedia.org/event/treaty-la-pointe-1854

Sweeney, J. M. (n.d.). Indigenous ceremonies and wisdom from an Ojibway teacher, accessible for any spiritual seeker [Review of One Drum: Stories and Ceremonies for a Planet, by R. Wagamese]. Spirituality and Practice. https://www.spiritualityandpractice.com/book-reviews/view/29069/one-drum

Tapia, R. (2021, April 22). *Preserving and Protecting Mother Earth. Partnership with Native Americans*. Native Partnership.

http://blog.nativepartnership.org/preserving-and-protecting-mother-earth/

Taylor, C. J. (2004). *Peace Walker: The legend of Hiawatha and Tekanawita*. CM Reviews. https://www.cmreviews.ca/cm/vol11/no6/peacewalker.html

Taylor, L., Willies-Jacobo, L., & Dixon, S. D. (2006). Cultural Dimensions in Child Care. *Encounters with Children (Fourth Edition): Pediatric Behavior and Development* (pp. 44–71). Mosby. https://doi.org/10.1016/b0-32-302915-9/50007-0

Tecumseh's Confederation. (n.d.). Ohio History Central. https://ohiohistorycentral.org/w/Tecumseh%27s_Confederation

Texas General Land Office. (2016, October 27). *Nine years a captive—the story of Herman Lehmann*. Save Texas History. https://medium.com/save-texas-history/nine-years-a-captive-the-story-of-herman-lehmann-61396e2ff78a

The Articles of Confederation (simplified): Approved by all 13 states between 1777 and 1781, (1781). chrome-extension://efaidnbmnnnibpcajpcglclefindmkaj/https://www.cde.state.co.us/cosocialstudies/simplifiedversions

The Legend of Chief Tamanend. (n.d.). Tamanend Middle School. https://www.cbsd.org/Page/3346

The Mescalero Apache Story. (n.d.). Inn of the Mountain Gods. Retrieved October 19, 2022, from https://innofthemountaingods.com/the-mescalero-apache-story/

The Ojibwe People. (n.d.). Minnesota Historical Society. https://www.mnhs.org/fortsnelling/learn/native-americans/ojibwe-people

Thompson, A. (2018, September 12). *Ojibwe women walk to protect sacred water*. ICT. https://indiancountrytoday.com/archive/ojibwe-women-walk-to-protect-sacred-water

3.17: Cherokee women. (2020, September 6). LibreTexts: Humanities. https://human.libretexts.org/Bookshelves/Literature_and_Literacy/Book%3A_Becoming_America_-_An_Exploration_of_American_Literature_from_Precolonial_to_Post-Revolution/03%3A_Revolutionary_and_Early_National_Period_Literature/3.17%3A_Cherokee_Women#:~:text=On%20September%208%2C%201787%2C%20Katteuha

Tikkanen, A. (2021). *Haida: People*. In Encyclopædia Britannica. https://www.britannica.com/topic/Haida

Tikkanen, A. (2022a, May 25). *Paula Gunn Allen: American Author and Scholar*. Encyclopedia Britannica. https://www.britannica.com/biography/Paula-Gunn-Allen

Tikkanen, A. (2022b). *Shawnee: People*. In Encyclopædia Britannica. https://www.britannica.com/topic/Shawnee-people

Tolles, F. B. (2022). *William Penn*. In Encyclopædia Britannica. https://www.britannica.com/biography/William-Penn-English-Quaker-leader-and-colonist/Founding-and-governorship-of-Pennsylvania

Van Winkle, I. (n.d.). *White Indian Herman Lehmann lived in two worlds, yet in neither*. Wk Current. https://wkcurrent.com/white-indian-herman-lehmann-lived-in-two-worlds-yet-in-neither-p974-71.htm

Vaughan, C. (2017, March 1). *The incredible legacy of Susan La Flesche, the first Native American to earn a medical degree*. Smithsonian Magazine. https://www.google.com/url?q=https://www.smithsonianmag.com/his

tory/incredible-legacy-susan-la-flesche-first-native-american-earn-medical-degree-
180962332/&sa=D&source=docs&ust=1666890439749168&usg=AOvVaw1-3QO3OR9sPrLPI8I0MHz_

Vision Quest. (2016). In Encyclopædia Britannica.
https://www.britannica.com/topic/Vision-Quest

Wallenfeldt, J. (2022a). *Quanah Parker: Native American Leader.* In Encyclopædia Britannica.
https://www.britannica.com/biography/Quanah-Parker

Wallenfeldt, J. (2022b). *Mohawk.* In Encyclopædia Britannica.
https://www.britannica.com/topic/Mohawk

Weiser, K. (2020, February). *Native American Rituals and Ceremonies.* Legends of America. https://www.legendsofamerica.com/na-ceremonies/

Welcoming Baby; Birth rituals provide children with a sense of community, culture. (2005, May 21). Parent Map.
https://www.parentmap.com/article/welcoming-baby-birth-rituals-provide-children-with-sense-of-community-culture

Who Was Bill Reid? (n.d.). Bill Reid Gallery of Northwest Coast Art.
https://www.billreidgallery.ca/pages/about-bill-reid

Wiencke, G. (n.d.). *Chief Tamanend.* Upper Southampton Township. https://www.ustwp.org/government/boards-commissions/historical-advisory-board/chief-tamanend/

William Henry Harrison: The 9th president of the United States. (n.d.). The White House. https://www.whitehouse.gov/about-the-white-house/presidents/william-henry-harrison/

Williams, K. (2021, November 26). *What is a shaman? Types, talents & examples.* Study.com. https://study.com/learn/lesson/what-is-a-shaman.html

Winona LaDuke. (2021, April). National Women's History Museum. https://www.womenshistory.org/education-resources/biographies/winona-laduke

Young adult books about coming of age as Native Americans. (n.d.). Igniting Writing. http://ignitingwriting.com/audiobooks/young-adult-books-about-coming-of-age-as-native-america

Made in the USA
Las Vegas, NV
26 October 2023

79692275R00059